D0175238

CP ✓

The Truth about Cheating

Also by M. Gary Neuman

Helping Your Kids Cope with Divorce the Sandcastles Way
Emotional Infidelity: How to Affair-Proof Your Marriage
and 10 Other Secrets to a Great Relationship
How to Make a Miracle: Finding Incredible Spirituality in Times
of Struggle and Happiness

The Truth about Cheating

Why Men Stray and What You Can Do to Prevent It

M. GARY NEUMAN

WILEY

John Wiley & Sons, Inc.

HIGH PLAINS LIBRARY DISTRICT
GREELEY, CO 80634

Copyright © 2008 by GKN Corporation. All rights reserved

Published by John Wiley & Sons, Inc., Hoboken, New Jersey
Published simultaneously in Canada

No part of this publication may be reproduced, stored in a retrieval system, or transmitted in any form or by any means, electronic, mechanical, photocopying, recording, scanning, or otherwise, except as permitted under Section 107 or 108 of the 1976 United States Copyright Act, without either the prior written permission of the Publisher, or authorization through payment of the appropriate per-copy fee to the Copyright Clearance Center, 222 Rosewood Drive, Danvers, MA 01923, (978) 750-8400, fax (978) 646-8600, or on the web at www.copyright.com. Requests to the Publisher for permission should be addressed to the Permissions Department, John Wiley & Sons, Inc., 111 River Street, Hoboken, NJ 07030, (201) 748-6011, fax (201) 748-6008, or online at http://www.wiley.com/go/permissions.

Limit of Liability/Disclaimer of Warranty: While the publisher and the author have used their best efforts in preparing this book, they make no representations or warranties with respect to the accuracy or completeness of the contents of this book and specifically disclaim any implied warranties of merchantability or fitness for a particular purpose. No warranty may be created or extended by sales representatives or written sales materials. The advice and strategies contained herein may not be suitable for your situation. You should consult with a professional where appropriate. Neither the publisher nor the author shall be liable for any loss of profit or any other commercial damages, including but not limited to special, incidental, consequential, or other damages.

For general information about our other products and services, please contact our Customer Care Department within the United States at (800) 762-2974, outside the United States at (317) 572-3993 or fax (317) 572-4002.

Wiley also publishes its books in a variety of electronic formats. Some content that appears in print may not be available in electronic books. For more information about Wiley products, visit our web site at www.wiley.com.

Library of Congress Cataloging-in-Publication Data:

Neuman, M. Gary.
  The truth about cheating: why men stray and what you can do to prevent it / M. Gary Neuman
      p. cm.
    Includes index.
    ISBN 978-0-470-11463-6 (cloth)
      1. Adultery. 2. Men—Psychology. 3. Men—Sexual behavior. I. Title.
  HQ806.N48   2008
  306.73'6081—dc22

                                                                        2008017674

Printed in the United States of America

10 9 8 7 6 5 4 3 2

For Fred Jonas, a teacher of unparalleled kindness, wisdom, and humility

CONTENTS

ACKNOWLEDGMENTS

Linda Shore, Ph.D., for answering every one of my calls, solving my problems, and pointing me in the right direction for my national research.

Professor Malky Zacharawitz, Ph.D., for her time and assistance in developing the survey questionnaire. She was the first person I went to and with excellent reason. Thank you, Malky, for listening and providing direction to my research.

Mary Anne Gorlen, Ph.D., for her assistance in reviewing my research survey and methods.

Alvaro Domenech, LCSW, for his time and effort assisting me with collecting and calculating data. Your professionalism and willingness to go the extra mile for this study is much appreciated.

Carol Mann, my agent. It's incredibly refreshing to work with someone who still does business on a handshake. Thanks for believing in this project and finding it a home. Your professionalism is unmatched.

My editor, Tom Miller. Thanks for your outstanding suggestions and reorganization of the book. Now it finally flows, and your talent really shows.

My copy editor, Roland Ottewell, and production editor, Rachel Meyers, for making this book proper.

All of the friends who took the time to help me with this project in ways large and small: Lynn and Sheldon Hanau, Rochelle Malek,

Robin Landers and Rick Hirsch, Allan Rosenthal, Karen Hader, Marty and Ellen Zeiger, Karen and Peter Cooper, Moshe Lehrfield, Nancy and Marty Engels, and Vicki Lansky. Each of you helped immeasurably, and your efforts and interest are appreciated.

Sandy Rosenblum, Esq., for your kindness and extraordinary efforts on my behalf, "included but not limited to . . ."

And on a personal note . . .

Melisa, who makes it all look so easy. Words are too limited to express the one soul we share. On a practical level, thank you for your insightful additions throughout the book, especially to chapter 8, and for your overall review. Thank you for your patience, your goodness, your kindness, and the passionate spirit you bring to our lives.

My kids, Danny, Pacey, Michael, Esther, and Yehuda. You guys are the greatest blessings a dad could imagine. Each of you adds immeasurably to my life. You are so kind and giving and so much fun to be around.

To everyone in the Neuman and Simons clan. I am supported by all of you and wouldn't be anywhere if it were not for each one of you. Thanks for the strength you give me every day.

My sister, Jill. Thanks for your overall review and suggestions for chapter 8. Your careful review of the manuscript is much appreciated.

Bonnie, for being the smartest person we know and being willing to use your powers for good.

To all the men and women who shared their thoughts and experiences, conflicts and struggles. I hope I've honored your disclosures with respect and that others can benefit and grow from your participation in this book.

The Truth about Cheating

PART ONE

Why and How
Men Cheat

1

This Book Will Change Your Marriage

This book is for every wife who wants to know what she can do to create a solid marriage. My research will show you the inside perspective on all husbands—the ones who cheat and the ones who don't—in order to let you know what most men are incapable of expressing themselves. By reading this book, you can learn from the men I've studied what you can do to build a meaningful, committed marriage.

As a marriage counselor, I have spent much of the last two decades watching marriages unfold, but my impulse to write this book derived from one particular experience. During one of my appearances on *Oprah*, I helped women whose husbands had cheated and left them for other women. The cheating men were firefighters who assisted the widows of fallen comrades and later began affairs with them. I realized on that show that cheating can happen in the most unlikely circumstances, even if the original intentions are well-meaning.

Fidelity Facts

How many husbands really cheat? Is it possible your husband is cheating? Could he be on his way? The results of studies are spread widely, suggesting that anywhere from 22 to 70 percent of husbands cheat on their wives. Many suggest the current acceptable statistic is that roughly half of all men have had affairs. Ruth Houston, the founder of infidelityadvice.com, says that anywhere from 38 to 53 million men in the United States have cheated on their wives. In other words, nearly one in every three couples will be affected by an affair. You may be unsure whether you and your husband are one of those couples, or you may confidently shake your head and be like so many who never imagined such a possibility.

I'm not sure how confident you should be that your husband would never cheat, though. According to my research, 69 percent of husbands who cheated never considered it a possibility. The rest who thought they might do it either told their wives they never would or cleverly avoided the topic.

Think your husband will confess if he's already done it? Extremely unlikely. Cheating men rarely do. Without being questioned, a mere 7 percent admitted to their wives that they had cheated. And unfortunately, few men admit to it even after multiple questioning. Shockingly, 68 percent never admit to cheating or only do so after their wives have concrete evidence of the affairs.

You may have heard that the Internet has swelled the ranks of cheating men. I'm not so sure. Keep in mind that back as far as 1953 Alfred Kinsey learned that 50 percent of husbands had had at least one affair by the time they were forty years old. Clearly the Internet has made cheating easier by helping men find women who are willing to have affairs with them and allowing them to hide those affairs. No longer does a man have to pretend that he is single or on his way to divorce in order to jump into bed with another woman.

Private Affairs is an online dating site that targets users looking for extramarital relationships, or EMRs. Another service, the Ashley Madison Agency, which boasts the motto "When monogamy becomes monotony," has 1.03 million members as of this book's printing and claims that its membership doubles annually. A German company, Perfect Alibi, claims to provide 350 clients a month with handy cover stories for cheating, such as bogus invitations to weekend business seminars.

William's Story: Cheating Trips

William was a manager at an international company. He traveled to multiple destinations every month for years, but it had nothing to do with business.

"I learned from a friend about the idea of creating trips regularly that sounded like business trips. I knew I could get caught if I said I was going on planes and then didn't, so I'd say I had to go to our offices in a different city, about a three-hour drive away. I'd only drive about an hour to see the woman I had an affair with for a few years. My wife never suspected and since she called me only on my cell phone, I never worried about her figuring things out through the office. Besides, I had the kind of flexibility at work that as long as I clocked in and did my job, they didn't care which office I was at."

In retrospect, William felt quite remorseful for his behavior. "Now that I think about it, I did feel bad especially when I'd return home and my wife would be nice to me because I was away and had such a hard trip. Oddly, it was really the only time we connected and I felt like she was being especially nice, so it was working for me on many different levels." William never told his wife about his affairs. It was only because of a car lease letter indicating the odometer reading that his wife was eventually tipped off. She confronted him with the facts but William maintained his innocence.

The message is clear. Now more than ever, it is worth learning what you can do to develop a marriage that is safe from infidelity. After being a marriage counselor for over twenty years and the author of multiple books and manuals on marriage and divorce, I have discovered how you can. I decided to write a book to solve the cheating problem the day I was contacted by a television station to comment on a book that asked women all kinds of questions about their cheating husbands, from warning signs the men sent to the reasons why they cheated. I wondered why people were only talking to wives about why their husbands cheat. Wouldn't it make more sense to ask the guys? As I searched the journal literature for answers that I could use for the interview, I was astounded by what I found—not a whole lot.

The issue of cheating is enormous to any marriage because it involves the most necessary ingredient of any relationship—trust— and yet the psychological world was far from offering a collective voice about how to avoid cheating. I felt that it was time to provide a well-researched response.

Getting Answers to Vital Questions

This book will lead you through the complex maze of the mind of the married man and offer you real answers to the big infidelity questions. Is it all about sex? What are the signs men say they're giving that show they are close to or already cheating? Will they tell you if they cheated? Do cheating men feel guilty about their actions? What do they say they're missing in their marriage and what could they and their wives have done to avoid it all? What do they say their mistresses were offering that their wives were not?

You can avoid a broken heart with clear answers. I've been helping people find their own solutions for over twenty years. Marriage counselors have a way of making the unclear and unknown seem rather obvious. We have to—we're good listeners, and after all the listening we begin to develop a sense of what works and what fails. We then parlay it into our own tips, advice, and theories and send that message to every person who asks for our help.

I wanted clarity. I recognize that we have a life outside of our marriage and we don't have all day to ruminate over making our marriage better. In this book, you will find the small number of areas that a wife could put her attention to. After all is said and done, you'll leave this book behind with a clear knowledge of what you should focus on in order to create a rock-solid marriage. Then you'll be able to follow through on your own. And don't worry—you won't be asked to do it all and be perfect in every area of your relationship.

The Research

I contacted a friend, a college professor, to help me in my quest. With the aid of many men and women and my own personal consideration, I created a forty-two-question survey that my friend improved into something that would give us all clear answers to the big mysteries about infidelity.

You may wonder how I could find cheating men who would be honest with me. I drew on a few different parts of the population in order to create a well-rounded study. I had two main sources for participants. In Miami, divorcing parents must attend a mandatory class that I was fortunate enough to be able to help develop many years ago. Another therapist on my research team and I took the opportunity to privately interview men from these classes. I found a plethora of men willing and able to share their many thoughts and stories.

Every interview was a learning experience for me. There were some strange moments: once I was reviewing a question about lying and the man told me to keep my voice down. "My wife is right over there and she still doesn't know," he said.

These men talked to me, another man, honestly because they would never see me again. I didn't know their names. I began to realize that I had a diverse group of men who could teach me and others a great deal. In order to create a well-rounded study, I also worked with an international online survey firm specializing in a wide variety of medical and psychological research. Men from forty-eight different states completed the questionnaires. There were also a handful of other surveys gathered from other research team members.

Each man chose one of two surveys to complete—"if you are having or ever had a physical infidelity," or "if you never had a physical infidelity." To get real answers, I had to go beyond cheating men. I wanted to truly find indicators for why men cheat, and I had to compare them to those of men who do not cheat. The men in both groups mirrored the percentages of the cultural, ethnic, and racial diversity of the U.S. population. Throughout the book I will clue you in to the responses of noncheating men as they relate to answers we discuss.

Ultimately, my study comprised two hundred men—one hundred cheaters and one hundred noncheaters who successfully completed the interviews and questionnaires. In total, I collected 25,500 individual responses.

How to Use This Book

My work is dedicated to helping you learn and change in ways that will significantly benefit *both* you and your husband.

In part two of this book, I'll share my Inner Voice Recognition Formula with you so that you will have a way to understand your challenge and make sensible, worthwhile changes. How often in life can you work to make changes and know that they will get you the result you want? Hardly ever. Being successful is your big motivation. There is nothing harder than change, especially in the world of emotions and love. But for every change you make, you'll be working toward the goal of a faithful husband.

You may be wondering what good it is if your husband doesn't read and make the changes with you. In this book, the men give you control by saying, "Had such and such happened, not only would we not have cheated, but we would have responded and been better husbands in general."

I'm Not Blaming the Victim

As you read on you might be wondering, "Why are you telling me all this? Tell him. He's the culprit." When I write about men and the aspects of their marriage that helped contribute to their cheating, I am by no means saying that the fact that they found flaws in their marriage gave them the right to. What they did was wrong, a clear breach of trust and the spoken rules of marriage.

But believe it or not, this doesn't usually mean that the cheating men didn't love their wives. I didn't meet a single cheater who was in any way cavalier about his actions. In fact, not a single one wanted to do it again and each one wished he could take it all back. All of the cheating men had some remorse and accountability even if they felt their wives' behavior was a strong factor in their infidelity.

So take this book in the only way it's meant—to empower you in your desire to have the marriage you want. I've written this book because I've seen the pain that women have endured when their husbands cheat as well as their suffering when their marriages are failing. You can make changes on your own that will create a safe, meaningful marriage.

The Stories

Throughout the book are personal stories that were shared with me during the interviews for this research. Identifying facts have been altered to protect privacy, but the feelings and issues are very much true. You will also read about many women who informally shared their own stories about their marriages, some of them knowing their husbands had cheated on them. Beyond these real stories, I have merged some as composites. I do not share the stories of clients who see me therapeutically, so any similarity between the stories in this book and those of people I have counseled is purely coincidental.

The Quick Action Program

Throughout the book, you'll find steps you can follow in my Quick Action Program. These concise focus points, suggested behaviors and schedules, and exercises will help you turn the knowledge and suggestions from this book into tangible improvements in your marriage. I created the Quick Action Program based on what we learned from the husbands who took the survey. Following the steps of the program will greatly diminish the chances that your spouse will cheat and at the same time will help create a more meaningful and intimate relationship.

Let's Find the Answers

During my research, when my determination got the best of me, often in the wee hours of the morning, I came to repeat a favorite phrase to myself: *the paralysis of analysis*. When conducting research, you always feel there is so much more you could've done with your study. As a result, you risk spending your time constantly tweaking your survey and gathering further information but never ending up with any clear and final results. I was determined to avoid this fate. My study needed to be clear and concise with precise direction. That goal was the primary focus that drove the study.

However, statistics are a lot about averages. They don't dictate how your husband will behave in an exact way. Among the husbands we surveyed, 12 percent of cheating men said that their wives' actions or inactions had nothing to do with their cheating. If your husband falls into this minority, you will not be able to influence the outcome.

The odds are, though, that you have a husband like the vast majority of respondents, the 88 percent who believe their cheating was linked to some significant dissatisfaction in their marriage.

Now, let's find the answers and take action. You will find some of the questions I used in my research with cheating men below. Please try to imagine how the cheating husbands answered and fill in your guesses. I'll reveal how the men responded in chapter 2. Remember that the men taking the survey had already cheated, and few had ever been in individual counseling. Don't think like a therapist, don't respond in the way a woman might answer, and don't guess as a way of compensating for what you've already been told will be the results. I want this to be a very personal activity so forget about trying to get it right and instead go with what you really feel the cheating men would say. That will be the best way of learning something helpful.

QUESTIONNAIRE

Why Do Men Cheat?

Can you read the minds of cheating men? Fill in the blanks with your guesses for how the men who have cheated on their wives answered these questions. For questions 1 through 10, each response should be a percentage value so that your answers add up to 100 percent.

1. The issues that figured into my infidelity can best be summed up as:

    _____ An unsatisfying sexual relationship with my wife outweighed the emotional dissatisfaction in our relationship

_X_ Emotional dissatisfaction in the marriage outweighed the sexual dissatisfaction

_____ Both emotional dissatisfaction and an unsatisfying sexual relationship figured about the same

_____ Other factors unrelated to either sexual or emotional aspects of my marital relationship prompted the infidelity

2. These issues factored into my infidelity:

_____ Sexual dissatisfaction

_X_ Emotional dissatisfaction

_____ Other

3. These were the specific sexual issues that factored into my infidelity:

_____ Sex life with my wife was unsatisfying

_____ My wife had significantly neglected her appearance

_____ Sex with my wife was generally too infrequent

_X_ Other

4. These were the specific emotional issues that factored into my infidelity:

_____ Other aspects of my wife's life (e.g., children, career, community responsibilities, etc.) were more important to her than our relationship

 I could not communicate my feelings to my wife

_____ I felt underappreciated by my wife. She was not sufficiently thoughtful and caring toward me

_____ My wife and I no longer shared the same values and/or interests

_____ I felt emotionally disconnected from my wife

____ My wife often lost her temper and was frequently moody, angry, and/or hostile, etc.

____ Other

5. Through this infidelity, the woman I cheated with differed from my wife in the following areas:

____ She offered things sexually that my wife would never consider

____ She made me feel wanted, loved, and appreciated

____ She was more physically attractive than my wife

____ I felt more emotionally connected to her than to my wife

____ I felt we shared more common values and/or interests

_X_ I felt that I could communicate more openly

____ Other

6. Prior to the infidelity, my wife and I attempted marital therapy:

_X_ Fewer than three sessions

____ Three to ten sessions

____ More than ten sessions

7. I met the woman I had the infidelity with:

_X_ At work

____ In the neighborhood

____ While engaging in some activity of personal interest

____ On the Internet

____ Other

8. Feelings of guilt:

____ Were not experienced during my affair

____ Were only experienced at the onset of the affair

_____ Continued throughout the affair

__X__ Escalated as the affair continued

9. When I got married:

__X__ I never thought I would have an infidelity

_____ I thought it was a possibility that I would have an infidelity

10. Did you:

_____ Tell your wife about the infidelity without being questioned?

_____ Tell your wife after the first time you were questioned?

_____ Tell your wife only after being questioned multiple times?

__X__ Tell your wife only after she had evidence?

_____ Lie to your wife even after she had some evidence of a relationship but not hard evidence of actual sex?

_____ Not disclose the affair and she has not questioned you up to this point

11. What warning signs do you think you gave to your wife that hinted that you were involved in infidelity? (Men could check off all that apply. Guess the percentage of men who checked off each item.)

_____ Avoidance of contact

_____ Unexplainable purchases of gifts for my wife

__X__ More criticism of her

_____ Diminished sexual activity

_____ More time spent away from home

_____ Transfer of funds from accounts

__X__ More fights with my wife

_____ Other

2

The Real Reasons
Men Cheat

Now that you're familiar with the facts on infidelity, don't stick your head in the sand and hope it will never happen to you. It's time to learn what you can do to prevent your husband from ever cheating, and of course at the same time develop a fulfilling marriage for both of you. You'd like to believe it's the farthest thing from your husband's thoughts, and it may be, or it may be just for today. Among the men who cheated, 69 percent never thought it was even a possibility that they would cheat on their wives. It's not something that had necessarily been planned for a long time. Maybe you don't think it'll happen because, after all, you think you'd never do it yourself. And then you remember what you've been trained to believe: men are really, really sexual and always looking, thinking, and fantasizing, and a woman's sexuality works quite differently. The assumption is that men cheat because they're wired to have sex with many women, spread their seed, or whatever the theory du jour is. A recent book on the female brain by the University of California psychiatrist Dr. Louann Brizendine revealed that a man thinks about sex every fifty-two seconds while the subject tends to cross a woman's mind just once a day.

Maybe you've been convinced that an infidelity could happen, but if you're like most women you don't want to believe it and surely don't want to focus on it. Do you know why I think you'd rather not? Because, really, what are you going to do about it? That's the key problem. Everybody has his or her own idea of what causes men to cheat. Perhaps if you had a collective answer, a unified response from men about what you could do to ensure your husband's fidelity, you'd act on it.

My first goal was to decide once and for all why men cheat. Is it really a biological thing? Are the cheaters wired to perpetuate the species and will therefore stray unless the sex at home is phenomenal? Are they emotionally dissatisfied at home? (Everyone tells you that men aren't very emotionally present beings.) Is it both factors or something completely different? Maybe it has nothing to do with the satisfaction of marriage. Men just cheat.

Statistically, I found that dissatisfaction has a very strong impact on the numbers of cheaters. Far fewer faithful men reported having pressing problems with their wives. The chances of your husband cheating go way down if he is feeling that things are going well in his marriage.

The Number One Reason Men Cheat

When the husbands were asked why they cheated, the most popular answer was emotional dissatisfaction. Turn back to the questionnaire and write this statistic next to your answer—48 percent of men said that was the primary issue that figured into their cheating. This result was perplexing considering men are regarded as the "less emotional" of the sexes. But yet for all of their sexual prowess, needs, and desires, the majority of men are not on the lookout for a new fantastic sex voyage with another woman. They are looking for emotional connection.

Cheating Men Confess: What Sort of Marital Dissatisfaction Contributed to My Infidelity?

48%—Primarily emotional dissatisfaction

32%—Equal emotional and sexual dissatisfaction

12%—Other/no dissatisfaction

  8%—Primarily sexual dissatisfaction

Overall:

59%—Dissatisfaction in marriage was emotional

29%—Dissatisfaction in marriage was sexual

12%—Other

Jason's Story: A No-Win Situation

Jason was a divorce attorney, of all things, and made a relatively good living. But bills were always an issue, and the two kids cost more every year. Somewhere along the line Jason found out that his wife didn't like him. And the funny thing was that he didn't necessarily disagree. "She had convinced me that I was an underachieving, insensitive husband," he told me with a shrug. "And so we kind of settled into this space where we'd be okay for a while and we could still have fun on vacation but if I didn't want to spend as much money on my kid's party, I was the bad guy. If I came home late because I was working like a dog, I was the bad guy. I couldn't win no matter which way I turned. After a while I figured I wasn't a very good husband. Regardless of what I did, I couldn't make my wife happy."

Jason stopped expecting the loving gestures he had received from his wife when they were falling in love and early on in the marriage. And as far as sex went, "We'd have it once

in a blue moon and then, ironically, it was like she was doing
me a big favor. It was like, 'Hurry up already.' And then if
I had any complaint for like the next month, she'd tell me
how good a wife she was because she gave me sex. I was so
frustrated that I figured this was the best it was ever going to
be. None of my friends had much better stories to tell. Their
wives didn't seem into it any more than mine."

Jason wasn't getting love from his marriage and perhaps
he didn't have a healthy approach to help his wife see
that. It could've been his fault for not communicating
things in a nonthreatening way, or perhaps he wasn't
willing to make time for fun and pleasure with his wife.
Everything changed the day Cheryl rented space in the
office next to him.

"Cheryl wasn't prettier than my wife, not a better person, not classier, none of that. Cheryl was a person who
liked to please people and she knew how to make you like
her. It's so pathetic when I think of it now, but she was
so complimentary and 'Let me do that for you, you've had
such a long day already' that I was hooked very quickly."

Cheryl quickly convinced Jason that he wasn't an awful
husband. Jason was feeling like a dog and Cheryl threw
him relatively small bones, which he chewed up.

"It just felt so good to hear I was sexy, accomplished. She
was starting out as an attorney so she really respected my
legal knowledge. Finally, someone was telling me how good
I was at what I do, sort of like it was when my wife and I
started out. My wife made me feel that I must be screwing
up because I wasn't writing enough articles for the legal
journals. It was always about what I should be doing to get
more business, make more money. And my wife may have
been partially right, of course. But Cheryl made me believe
that I was a fantastic lawyer and a great provider. She told

me she'd kill to have a large practice like mine. She worked her way through college, was the first woman in her family to go beyond college and get a law degree, so she had this enormous energy and determination to learn everything she could about law. I became a mentor in a way, and what can I say . . . it just felt too good."

Many cheating husbands shared Jason's sentiments. They had wives who sent the message that they were less than adequate husbands. I don't think the wives said it in so many words, but these men seemed to get that message because there was more conversation about what they were doing wrong than right. And I can't say that the women were wrong, either. Perhaps their husbands *were* insensitive, lazy, selfish, but somewhere along the line these men began to believe that their wives *defined* them this way. There was a distinct moment when they all seemed to have settled into an "I can't win" sort of place.

It's All about the Emotions, Not the Sex

I wrote a book called *Emotional Infidelity*, so the fact that emotional dissatisfaction was the number one reason why men cheat wasn't a huge surprise to me, although I wasn't sure that the men who cheated would see it this way. But I never anticipated how few men would say that sexual dissatisfaction outweighed emotional dissatisfaction — *only 8 percent*. When I do an Internet search for information about why men cheat, I always seem to get "sex" as the main answer. "For most, it's a sexual thing" (womansavers.com). "Statistically speaking, men cheat for a single primary reason: sex" (infidelityfacts.com). I figured that the men I interviewed would immediately go to that answer first, if not most of the time then at least a large part of the time. But they didn't. They spoke in a loud, singular voice. For 92 percent of the men living in the United States, cheating is not primarily about sex.

I was curious to know what specifically were these emotional issues. What exactly did these men feel they were missing in their marriage? And here again is one of my major surprises. When I've asked a marriage counselor or a woman why there is infidelity or divorce, the number one answer I get is communication. I thought for sure that cheating men would list communication as the number one source of their emotional dissatisfaction as well. It was on the list of choices. I also thought that a close second would be the wife's moods and temper. After all, I read all the time about women and those blasted hormonal shifts that drive husbands crazy. Was I wrong!

Appreciation Is Key

Among all of the possible causes of emotional dissatisfaction the most common answer was, "I felt underappreciated by my wife. She was not sufficiently thoughtful and caring toward me." This response made up 37 percent of the emotional problems for these men. Consider also that "I felt emotionally disconnected from my wife" represented 17 percent of the problems they felt. Together, these two answers that clearly relate to their wives' appreciation, thoughtfulness, and emotional connection represent 54 percent of the emotional dissatisfaction that cheating men believed helped lead them into the arms of another woman. The feeling of under-appreciation and lack of thoughtfulness far outweighed any other choice on the list:

- Lack of communication—11%
- My wife and I no longer share the same values—10%
- My wife often lost her temper—12%

Emotional disconnection? Appreciation? Doesn't that sound like a woman is talking? The big lie we keep hearing over and over again is women are the emotional ones, whereas men are like rocks, doing their thing, needing only lots of sex to be happy. Stop believing these myths or else the odds of your husband cheating will dramatically rise.

This doesn't mean that the answer is to run to your husband and talk about mushy stuff. One thing I've learned from my experience with cheating men is that classical talking is not the best way they relate. So I will clearly discuss all the things you can do to make sure your husband does feel appreciated, cared for, and emotionally connected.

One cheating husband told me a story about one occasion when he got up at 5:30 A.M. to make preparations for a surprise birthday breakfast for his wife. They had been in a bad sort of way and he thought this would be a good gesture to show her he heard her complaints—his peace offering. Well, needless to say, it didn't go according to plan. His two little kids wanted to make popcorn for Mommy so he microwaved it . . . a bit too long. By the time he caught it, the kitchen was smoking, and not just any old smell, but that burnt popcorn stench. The smoke alarm began to blare and his wife was awoken to chaos at 6:11 A.M. on her birthday. Understandably, she was pissed. But the husband became so angry that she couldn't even take a moment to appreciate his good intentions that he left the house that morning and didn't return until the evening. It was that day that he had his first sexual meeting with another woman. He hasn't told his wife yet.

Despite this tale, don't worry that one mistake will throw your husband into the arms of another. Clearly, this man's marriage was faltering for some time. If only you could see the forlorn look on his face as he told me this story. He didn't want this to happen and he was not proud of his cheating. He just wanted to do the right thing and instead seemed to be driving his wife crazy—a scenario that I've heard repeated often during my study. Believe me, he might not have been someone I'd want to live with. But his point was clear: he tried, and even though he screwed up, he wanted to show he cared through trying. Men need to hear how wonderful they are and to be appreciated for what they do right. Just how to accomplish that is a trick we'll get to.

Women commonly misinterpret their husband's bravado as confidence and ego. Remember the bully in school really feeling small inside so he needs to feel bigger by picking on little people, or the guy who has to smoke the really big cigar? Just because men *seem* like they're strong and powerful doesn't mean they don't regularly question themselves or worry about their skills and abilities. They may not *talk* emotionally, may not say things like, "When you speak that way it makes me feel . . ." but make no mistake, they are emotional beings who are looking for warmth, kindness, and appreciation.

As women have gained more respect in our culture, men have diminished somewhat. You're not a "good" man anymore if you make a good living and coach your kid's football team. No, no. The real question is, do you change diapers? Do you skip some Sunday football to be at your in-laws' family barbecue? Do you plan a date night and arrange a babysitter? How about some household cleaning? My point is only that men tend to get less appreciation because they're expected to do more than ever before.

Whenever I counsel a couple, I do an appreciation exercise with them early on in our therapy. Each partner is given a pad and asked to write all of the things that he/she appreciates about the other. Invariably, the list is very short. After reviewing the list of about two to three things I ask the simple

---

Appreciation Exercise

Women often feel their husbands don't deserve to be appreciated for things they are expected to do. Men's roles have shifted to include many more expectations than ever before. All of us, yourself included, want and desire appreciation for our efforts no matter what.

Create an appreciation list for your husband—even for things he's expected to do. Verbalize or show your appreciation with a thoughtful gesture at least three times a week.

questions: "Doesn't he hold down a good job, isn't he an attentive father, doesn't he make time for vacation?" And it's always the same answer: "But he's supposed to do that." Somehow, we've concluded that whatever is expected of our spouse is not worthy of appreciation. As the bar gets raised, appreciation diminishes. As a woman appreciates her husband less and less and focuses on what he does not do more and more, her motivation to be "thoughtful and caring" understandably decreases and it's an immediate step toward a man feeling emotionally disconnected from his wife. This logical process makes up 54 percent of the problem that contributes to cheating, the men say.

Cheating men wanted their wives to give to them in a host of ways, whether it be a neck massage, initiating sex, buying them their favorite CD, cooking a special dessert, saying how wonderful they were, or any other thoughtful gesture. These men often admitted that they needed to do the same for their wives. But in their minds, the main contributor to their cheating was that they had come to feel that thoughtful gestures were sorely lacking.

However, many cheating men told me that they don't want their wives to tell them daily that they are hard workers with simple comments that they'd find condescending—they want their wives to *show* them through gestures that they are appreciated. They want their wives to really understand how hard they are trying to do the right things.

And here was the first of many key elements to turning around cheating.

"I didn't know how to tell my wife. What was I going to say, 'Love me, tell me I look handsome, that I'm hot'? That's not me. She may want to hear it but I wanted her to do things that meant something to me and I probably wasn't so good at telling her. I mean I did but I didn't."

This cheating husband explained that he wanted more sex, more comments about how he turned her on, not just that he looked good. He wanted her to really celebrate with him when he did something positive at work, not just because it meant there was more money for the family but because she really appreciated how much energy and know-how it took him to get the job done. He didn't want her to just take his success for granted by implying that he was so smart, she knew he'd do it.

The Breadwinner Role

Men are largely raised to provide and protect. As far forward as society has moved in not placing people into categories just because of gender, men are still thought of as the ones primarily responsible for protecting and providing financially for the family. Appreciation for their work in this area is often missed by wives. Naturally, there are many women today who earn a significant part of the family income and therefore don't see how their husbands deserve greater appreciation than they do. I'm not in any way suggesting that you do not deserve great appreciation for your work outside the home if you are one of those wives. Yet for many women the pressure to generate income is less than for their husbands. I'm not talking about day-to-day energy or pressure but rather the overall social pressure that your husband has to bear. In most cases, a man is still going to be seen as the one primarily responsible for financially caring for his family. This pressure is huge regardless of how much income you bring to the table. Bottom line: if your family suffers financially, few people are going to look askance at you. Almost everyone is going to judge your husband negatively and infer that he has failed in some way even if you had a lot to do with the financial problems.

"I really thought I was going to be told that I was becoming partner," Joel said as he related a story that described how stuck he felt at work. "It was a big meeting in my mind. All of the partners were there and I'd been giving my heart and soul to this company for years. I thought I was going to keel right over when I got chewed out for every little thing for the last few years. Every expense report, every sick day, every everything was under scrutiny. Suddenly I find out my e-mails were being monitored, my company credit card was going to be cut, and one of the partners' snot-nosed nephews was now my new watchdog. I was to 'mentor' him so he could basically supervise me, learn what I do, and eventually take over my position. I was in shock. I left the meeting, went into the bathroom, and got so furious that I was going to walk right back into their partner meeting and quit. But then I thought of how we were right in the middle of our kitchen remodeling and expansion at home and I just knew I had to suck it up and figure out some other way to manage." Joel had to put up with a humiliating scenario, in his opinion, and if not for his serious obligation to financially support his family, he felt he would not tolerate the situation.

But where is the appreciation? Men need to be appreciated for fulfilling the responsibilities they have been learning since they were little. Learn to understand that your husband's ability to protect and provide for you is an identity that's been drilled into him forever. It doesn't mean he hasn't or won't be able to learn to identify himself in other crucial ways like being a loving husband to his wife and father to his kids. It just means that he needs to feel that you give him high marks in these areas. He wants you to tell him that you are thankful that you can live the lifestyle you do because of his hard work, that your kids can have a vacation, holiday presents, nice clothing, and so on because he works to make it happen. This takes nothing away from you or your need to feel appreciated by him. It just focuses you on one of the most significant areas of your husband's existence.

The Role Your Husband's Family and Friends Play in His Cheating

Ellen's Story: A Friend's Bad Influence

"I didn't know what to do. After all, Roger was his friend since childhood. I didn't like the way he behaved, but how was I going to tell my husband who he should and should not hang out with? What was the big deal if he went out to the bar or played softball with him on Sundays? I was a blind fool. But I know it now. Roger is finally out of our lives but he's made himself a part of our marital failure forever."

Ellen wasn't fond of her husband Jerry's closest childhood friend but put up with him for the sake of her husband. She didn't like Jerry's brother either but felt it wasn't her place to do anything about it. It was after her third child that she began to get suspicious and after a few months found out her husband was indeed cheating. She had no way to ever trust him again. But she learned from her husband that he had found his girlfriend while visiting clubs on South Beach that he likely would never have frequented had it not been for Roger, who had a way with women even though he was married for the second time.

Ellen hired a private investigator, who brought pictures to her of Jerry and the girlfriend dancing at the clubs. At first Jerry denied everything and just said he did dance at the clubs but it was what everyone did. His own brother, who was single and quite the ladies' man, went out with Jerry and Roger many times.

"Jerry made it seem like I was some dinosaur. Imagine my old-fashioned ways, not wanting my husband out dancing with strange women all hours of the night." Once Jerry finally admitted that he had cheated, he was remorseful and told Ellen he'd do anything to keep the family together. Ellen wanted to make it work but she surely didn't know how and never expected that she could trust him again. "I remember the night I told Jerry that it was over, really over, unless he swore to me that he'd have nothing to do with Roger again and that he'd only see his brother over at our house. Jerry went crazy, explaining that he was to blame, not his brother and best friend. Frankly, I knew he was to blame, but I was grasping at straws, some way to make myself feel better, to feel that there'd be some change that would give me hope of trusting my husband again. I couldn't remain married and worry every time he went out that he was cheating again."

Was Ellen grasping at straws? Your husband may have that one friend you can't stand because you think he's a cheater or a misogynist. Maybe the friend is single so it's okay for him to be out playing the field, but is it okay for your husband to go along for the ride? Does it make sense for you to impose on your husband to stop being friends with a close friend who is himself a cheater?

In the box below are the results of my research into the influence of friends and family on cheating.

The Influence of His Friends and Family

Faithful men who have close friends who have cheated—47%

Cheating men who have close friends who have cheated—77% (only 23% of cheating men did not have close friends who cheated)

Faithful men who have immediate family members who have cheated—33%

Cheating men who have immediate family members who have cheated—53%

Faithful men whose dads had or were suspected of cheating—28%

Cheating men whose dads had or were suspected of cheating—50%

Faithful men whose dads had multiple affairs—8%

Cheating men whose dads had multiple affairs—21%

One of the most overwhelming findings of my research came when I compared the two groups of men regarding their friends. I asked both groups if they were aware of close friends who had had an infidelity. When it came to cheating men, 30 percent more reported having these types of friends than faithful men did. Only 23 percent of cheating men did not have close friends who cheated. Remember that there were many faithful men who had close friends who cheated, which of course means that you could have a faithful man who maintains a close friendship with a cheating husband. But with such a dramatic difference, you'd want to think twice about looking the other way when it comes to your husband's cheating friends.

Our friends are far more influential than we probably believe. When you have close friends who cheat, it creates an atmosphere that makes cheating a part of everyday living. So why allow cheating to be a part of your social circle? Why create a culture of infidelity by hanging out with others who cheat? Wives beware. The innocent friendship can be dangerous.

Friendships can influence a great marriage, too. Friends matter. My own in-laws, who have been married for over four decades and still go out dancing together, claim that not one of their couple friends are divorced or mean to one another.

What are you supposed to do when your husband has a cheating friend? Few women will get a positive result by forbidding a version of Roger in their husband's life. But it's too important to ignore. At the very least, after registering your complaint to your husband, request that the friend come to your house to hang out with him or do your best to be around your husband and the friend when they are out. You can't stop them from talking about the friend's infidelity, but in this way you can limit your husband being taken for a ride down "Let's meet some girls" lane. You can also limit the conversation about infidelity and its permissiveness if you're around the relationship more often than not.

Ellen recounted that on one occasion Roger shared the horror stories of his infidelity and she thought perhaps it was good for her husband to hear. It didn't work that way for Jerry. Even if a friend shares that the infidelity was a bad idea, it still legitimizes cheating as a distinct possibility. If your husband is one in a group of cheating men, his social circle is sending him a strong message about the normality of infidelity. Do your best to impart this concern to your husband and look to socialize with couples who are committed to faithful relationships.

Along the same lines, you should also be worried if your husband's immediate family members are cheating. Whereas only 33 percent of faithful men said that they were aware of immediate family members having cheated, 53 percent of cheating men answered yes to the same. You might not be able to do anything about this. Can you tell your husband to stop talking to his father or brother because they cheated and you don't want him to learn from them? Not gonna happen. But you should be aware of the greater likelihood that your husband might cheat and therefore be more vigilant about creating a safe marriage.

What if His Dad Cheated?

"I was fifteen when I saw him with her." Pete was describing to me the first time he confirmed that his father was cheating on his stepmother. "I suspected, and of course my mom had told me that was the reason they broke up." Pete was at a McDonald's downtown with his girlfriend at the time. They were there on a high school trip when he saw his dad walk by on the sidewalk with the woman who was the interior designer for the house that they were remodeling. "I was totally caught off guard and I'll never forget how cool I played it. My girlfriend asked if I saw it—he had his arm around her—and I said they were just friends. But I knew. I never mentioned it to anyone but I hated her every time she'd come over. After a while, I guess it became obvious and my stepmother found out. How ironic that I ended up cheating with a woman (my attorney) who had become close to our family and also had been over to our house many times. My wife and kid had to feel the same way my stepmom and I felt."

Ironic? Far from it. In my study, fifty men who had cheated reported that their dad had or was suspected of having an infidelity. Compare that with only twenty-eight men from the faithful group who said the same. Plus, many more cheating men said their father had multiple infidelities, twenty-one of them to be exact, compared to eight men in the faithful group. When I asked each group how long their fathers had cheated, the faithful group reported an average of four years nine months. The cheating group? The average was twelve years. Not only did the men who cheated have a higher incidence of fathers who cheated than the faithful men and had more multiple affairs than the faithful men, but their affairs lasted an average of over seven years longer than those of the faithful men.

How Cheating Men Perceive Their Parents' Marriage

When men were asked how they perceived their parents' marriage, things became even more dramatic. Of cheating men, 49 percent said they perceived their parents' marriage as generally positive and 51 percent said they saw their parents' marriage as generally nega-tive and filled with much conflict. But 82 percent of faithful men reported seeing their parents' marriage as positive and only 18 percent saw Mom and Dad's marriage as negative.

Zack hadn't spoken to his dad for years. He was terribly angry at how his dad had treated his mom when he was a child. Soon after his parents' divorce when Zack was seventeen years old, he assumed the Daddy role in the house and became his mom's protector. "It was funny because as I grew up and cared for my mother, I learned that she was not such an easy person. I mean, she could really nag and get stuck on things. She'd drive me crazy and I'd scream at her. It ended up being the way I spoke to my wife after a while—she always told me how much she disliked the way I talked to her. After cheating on both of my first two wives I've learned that I was so ready to fight with them and see them as difficult. I'm not sure how it all would have been different if my parents didn't have such a crappy marriage, but I'm sure my adult relationship with women would have been much smoother."

Most of us don't want to believe that what happens to us as kids dictates our behavior as adults. We want to believe that the past is the past and we can't do anything about it now anyway so why stay stuck there. But we have to look back in order to look forward.

In many different ways what we experienced as kids—those "voices" in our past—can still have a great deal to do with our behavior now even if we're not hearing our actual parents today. When a boy is raised in a family culture that allows infidelity, it will dictate his feelings around that subject. You might argue that a cheating father isn't a culture, but it is in a way. Whether it's considered allowable or wrong, the family culture still normalizes infidelity. It's similar to the reality that children who come from divorced homes are more likely to divorce as adults. When their parents divorced, no one said, "Hip-hip hooray!" Most likely it was seen as a failure, but it still presented a reality, a culture of sorts.

Your husband's parents presented right and wrong to their children, and it was not all about what they said. The old adage "Do as I say, not as I do" is commonly known to be a crock. If your father-in-law cheated, your husband has been taught a lesson about cheating whether he wanted it or not. Likewise, if your father-in-law remained faithful, he too taught your husband a valuable lesson, one that diminishes the odds of his ever cheating on you. And the same goes for the marriage that your in-laws had when your husband was a child.

Find out more from your husband about your in-laws. If his father did cheat, for how long? How many times? You can't change your husband's past but you can be aware of it and spend extra time considering with him the messages he was sent. Don't start off by tell-ing him, "Your dad taught you that cheating was okay," because you'll come across as a presumptuous psychobabblish partner. Instead just try to learn about your husband's experience with it all. How did he find out, how old was he, did he discuss it with anyone in or outside the family? Just the ongoing discussion can work wonders to disrupt the idea implanted in his head that cheating happens to the best of us. Plus, one of the biggest compliments is to be curious about someone. As he shares this part of himself, you become a part of this world, the ancient world of his childhood, and it's no longer just about him and his family of origin. Now it's about you as well since you've implanted yourself as part of his childhood world.

Talk to him about his parents' marriage in general even if there was no cheating going on. Tread carefully. Don't be judgmental. Stay far away from "I can't believe they did that," and stay close to "Wow, how'd you manage through that?" The second statement is empower-ing to your husband and lets him know you want to be with him and that you appreciate the strength he used to get through some of his childhood crap.

Cynthia hated her father-in-law. She wasn't at all surprised when I shared this chapter's statistics with her. "I knew my father-in-law was a philanderer and I knew he was a pig. And it drove me crazy every time my husband defended him. His mother was no better. After a while, she decided if you can't beat 'em, join 'em, and they agreed to have an open marriage through my husband's teenage years and into college. They're still together although it's not open anymore, or at least that's what my husband tells me. I don't believe that man would ever stop cheating. He'll probably have a whole harem show up to his funeral."

Cynthia wasn't getting past her feelings about her in-laws anytime soon. But it all so infuriated her that she attacked them when she spoke about them with her husband, and that caused him to defend them. It didn't allow him to see her point that he must be careful not to carry on the same traits. Instead they just argued every time the subject came up, usually initiated by Cynthia. Even after she found out her husband was cheating on her, he still defended his parents and refused to believe that they had anything to do with his mistakes.

Children don't like to put down parents at any age. Our society teaches us to respect our parents and appreciate them, and even though many can joke that their parents are driving them crazy again, they'll still visit them for the holidays and be loving toward them. You can't just come at your in-laws and tear them apart in conversation with your husband. When attacked, men will react as Cynthia's husband did and defend their parents. Your place is to have discussions about parents in general, the good, the bad, and the ugly. Use childhood discussions as a way of connecting to your husband. The point is that the less judgmental you are, the more he'll feel comfortable talking with you about Mom and Dad. The less emotional you are about it (no "Aw, poor you"), the easier he'll be with sharing it. If you talk more emotionally about it than he wants to think of it, your husband will begin to cover up and start saying things like, "It wasn't that bad, actually, it made me stronger. It was good in the end." When those comments start flying, it's a good indicator you felt more emotional than he was comfortable with.

In my research, I wanted to find out how cheating men felt about their parents today. Did they get along with Mom and Dad or not? Somewhat telling was that most men even in the cheating group regarded their relationship with their parents as generally positive, 79 percent of them, leaving only 21 percent seeing their relationship with their parents as generally negative. But in the faithful group, 95 percent of the men felt good about their relationship with their parents, obviously leaving only 5 percent perceiving their relationship with Mom and Dad as negative. There's no doubt that a man's past will affect his future, at least in the area of whether or not he'll cheat on his wife.

What about His Coworkers and Acquaintances?

As far as coworkers and acquaintances go, the worry dips a bit. My study didn't show huge differences between cheating and faithful men when it came to coworkers and acquaintances. But it would be wise for you to recognize the concept that your husband's immediate world will likely have an impact on how he views cheating. He may say and think it's wrong, but with enough people around him who share intimate details about their infidelities, it's going to rub off on him, and that's the last thing you need. Talking about it might only get you so far. Developing friendships with other couples whom you feel are strongly faithful will probably be the wisest change you could make if these are your circumstances.

QUICK ACTION PROGRAM

Step One: Keep Tabs on His Friends and Family

1. Invite his friends and immediate family members into your home so that you can learn more about them. This tactic will also give you the advantage of becoming a part of the friendly energy your husband shares with these men. Sometimes wives dislike their husband's friends and choose to stay far away. However, we've learned that you've improved your odds of fidelity by knowing as much about his friends' lifestyles as possible without seeming overbearing.

2. If he has close friends who are cheaters, introduce him to new friends by going out with other couples. Often you meet new people through work or your children's schools, and those who seem to be having good marriages can serve as positive role models for both you and your husband. The more time he spends with new faithful men, the less significant his cheating friends become. This also avoids the difficult discussion of "I don't like your life-long friend and I want you to stop hanging out with him."

You can request that when he does spend time with a close friend who cheats, he does so in a healthy environment—your home, a restaurant for lunch, or a sporting event. You want to avoid his going to the bar, club, late dinners with this friend. Your husband should not witness his cheating friend flirting with women.

The Other Woman

Of the men I studied, 54 percent cheated with one woman, leaving a whopping 46 percent having multiple affairs. Forty-seven percent cheated for less than one year, 24 percent cheated between one and two years, 9 percent cheated between two and four years, and 20 percent cheated more than four years. The average time cheating men were married before having their first infidelity? Six years.

Ted's Story: The College Girlfriend

"I could never really explain to my wife why I felt so good with the other woman. She wanted to believe I was just the scum of the earth and nothing more." Ted had been married for eleven years when his college girlfriend moved to town. He hadn't seen her for fourteen years but admittedly had thought about her from time to time and wondered how she was. He'd learned that she had gotten married and widowed soon after. After his old girlfriend she became his mistress, Ted's wife was incensed and felt Ted lacked self-control, plain and simple.

"Maybe she was right. I shouldn't have done this to her, to my kids, even to Sheila, the woman I cheated with. But when I was caught, my wife was so infuriated that she never wanted to find out why it all really happened. Basically, I was a horrible human being who threw away a good thing—my wife and kids. But I don't see it that way.

I spent months in therapy understanding myself, crying, and apologizing to my wife. And when it was my turn to talk about what wasn't going right for me, it was always the same thing. 'Don't use it as an excuse.'

"The way I felt with Sheila was so totally different than with my wife. I walked into Sheila's apartment and she wanted to be nice to me. Simple things, offer me a massage, espresso, just sit and want to hear about my day. We didn't have sex for a long time but frankly I felt like I was having sex all along. The sex was only great because of how much she loved me.

Ted described what a lot of cheating men have thought. What they miss in their wives they get from their mistresses. It makes sense. But what was it that they really felt with these mistresses that had this incredible power over them? Was it that the mistresses were so much more physically attractive, or perhaps the men could communicate with them in a way they just couldn't with their own wives? Maybe the sex was just so good because these mistresses knew some things every wife should know? Not at all.

Surprisingly, only 12 percent of cheating men said that the mistress was more physically attractive than their wives. This means that 88 percent felt their wives were as physically attractive as the mistress or more so. No one says you shouldn't work on your body and outward physical appearance, but don't do it because you think that's going to stop your husband from cheating, because there are many better places to put your energy.

The best place to put your energy? You might have guessed it by now. My research showed that the number one way the other woman differed from the cheating man's wife was that she made him feel wanted, loved, and appreciated—28 percent.

So we've seen it from both sides of the spectrum. The men stated that emotional issues were the number one problem in the marriage and now put forth emotional issues as the number one gain from the infidelity. Nine percent also reported "I felt emotionally connected" as the primary difference. So we could comfortably say that 37 percent of the cheating men felt the primary difference between the wife and the mistress was emotional pleasure.

Could these men communicate more openly with their mistress? Only 12 percent said so.

Was it about sharing more common values and/or interests? Only 11 percent felt this way.

Was it sex? The answer "Offered me things sexually my wife wouldn't" received a 22 percent response, which is not large but was the number two answer. This finding fits with what the men were saying about their wives. These men were primarily seeking an emotional relationship with their wives, and when they were unable to find it or continue it—for many reasons that they took a great deal of responsibility for—they found it outside of their marriage. Sex came along for the ride and that was better as well.

As part of my research, I asked a separate question about sex with the mistress. I asked whether the sex "was not much different (physically) than the sex with my wife," or "was much different than the sex with my wife."

Sixty-eight percent of the men said the sex was much different. This result was fascinating to me because only 8 percent of these same men listed sexual dissatisfaction as the primary problem in their marriage at the time of the cheating.

So even though these cheating men are not on the prowl for better sex, even though they're not looking for better-looking women and often don't find anyone better-looking, even though on average the other woman offers things that the wife doesn't 22 percent of the time, the sex was much different for 68 percent of the men.

Was the sex better because the mistresses had some skill that the wives did not? Unlikely. Keep in mind that most of them weren't any better-looking or in better shape than the wives. It would be an absurd conclusion to think that 68 percent of the mistresses went to a great sex school or had something that gave them the edge. More likely, the answer is that the emotional part of the relationship created a better sexual relationship. There could be many reasons for that. Surely we've learned that emotions drive the sexual relationship long-term. Were the mistresses more skilled emotionally than the wives? The greater likelihood is that the men were better able to receive love and connect with the women because of a host of possible reasons: their sense of lacking it at home, the right timing, the lack of stress in this new relationship that allowed only the good things to prevail.

It seems that every ounce of effort you put into the emotional part of your marriage will quickly translate to better sex as well. Developing an attitude of appreciation and kind gestures will strike a huge chord with your husband and make every part, emotional and physical, of your relationship different.

QUESTIONNAIRE

Is He Cheating?

No simple quiz can accurately take into account the unique circumstances inherent to every relationship. This quiz was developed based on the average couple's experience and the results reported in my study. It is meant to be the beginning of a conversation you may have with yourself and possibly your spouse. This is not a true diagnostic tool as much as a general baseline by which to measure your situation.

I believe that my husband:	Agree	Disagree	Strongly Agree	Strongly Disagree
1. Feels he can communicate well with me	☐	☒	☐	☐

	Agree	Disagree	Strongly Agree	Strongly Disagree
2. And I share the same values and/or interests	☒	☐	☐	☐
3. Feels I am caring and thoughtful toward him	☐	☐	☐	☒
4. Would say he feels appreciated by me	☐	☒	☐	☐
5. Feels emotionally connected to me	☐	☒	☐	☐
6. Thinks I lose my temper too much and would describe me as moody	☐	☐	☒	☐
7. Feels other aspects of my life (e.g., children, career, community responsibilities, etc.) take priority over our relationship	☒	☐	☐	☐
8. Finds me physically attractive	☒	☐	☐	☐
9. Would like to have sex more often	☒	☐	☐	☐
10. Finds the sex we have to be fulfilling	☒	☐	☐	☐
11. Has been avoiding contact with me more over the last month or longer (with no obvious reason— e.g., he's been traveling more than usual, been ill; if there is an obvious reason why he's avoiding contact more of late, answer "Disagree")	☐	☒	☐	☐

	Agree	Disagree	Strongly Agree	Strongly Disagree
12. Has spent more time away from home over the last month or more (with no obvious reason— e.g., he's been traveling more than usual; if there is an obvious reason why he's avoiding contact more of late, answer "Disagree")	☐	☐	☐	☒
13. Has become increasingly critical the last month or more	☒	☐	☐	☐
14. Has had diminished sexual activity with me over the last two months or more	☐	☒	☐	☐
15. Has purchased gifts for me lately with no explanation for them and this is unlike him	☐	☒	☐	☐
16. Has at least one very close friend who has cheated on his wife/girlfriend	☐	☒		
17. Has at least one immediate family member who has cheated on his wife/girlfriend	☒	☐		
18. Has a father who has cheated on his mother	☒	☐		
19. Has at least one coworker who has cheated	☒	☐		
20. Perceives his parents' marriage as generally positive	☐	☒	☐	☐

	Agree	Disagree	Strongly Agree	Strongly Disagree
21. Has a generally positive relationship with his parents	☐	☐	☐	☒
22. Has significant job-related pressures	☒	☐	☐	☐
23. Has significant financial stress	☒	☐	☐	☐
24. Has significant stress related to his or my family of origin	☒	☐	☐	☐
25. Attends organized religious services regularly	☐	☒	☐	☐

ANSWER SHEET
Circle the score that corresponds to your answer.

	Agree	Disagree	Strongly Agree	Strongly Disagree
1.	0	0	1	−1
2.	0	0	1	−1
3.	2	−2	3	−3
4.	3	−3	6	−6
5.	1	−1	2	−2
6.	0	0	−1	1
7.	0	0	−1	1
8.	0	0	1	−1
9.	−2	2	−4	4
10.	1	−1	2	−2
11.	0	0	−1	1
12.	−3	1	−6	2
13.	0	0	−1	1
14.	−2	0	−3	1
15.	0	0	0	0

	Agree	Disagree	Strongly Agree	Strongly Disagree
16.	−2	1		
17.	−1	1		
18.	−2	2		
19.	0	0		
20.	1	−1	2	−2
21.	0	0	1	−1
22.	0	0	0	0
23.	0	0	0	0
24.	0	0	0	0
25.	0	0	1	−1

If your score is in the range of +17 to +35, it is very unlikely your husband is cheating or will cheat on you. Keep doing what you're doing and apply the principles outlined in the book to make your marriage even better.

If you score in the range of −21 to +16, you're on shaky ground; you should be aware. Begin to cultivate a home culture of kindness, calmness, and appreciation. Slow it down. Make each other the focus. Eliminate the distractions that dilute intimacy. Have time for you so you can reenergize and develop your refreshed marital plan.

If your score is in the range of −22 to −42: crisis. He is at severe risk for cheating or already is cheating. Simultaneously work to improve the marriage as best you can while protecting yourself. Consider drastic measures from intensive marital therapy to conducting some surveillance as outlined in this book.

One caveat—regardless of your score, pay more attention to your risk factor if you checked "Strongly Agree" to both questions 12 and 14, as these are strong indicators of a marriage in trouble.

3

Warning Bells, Cheating Signals, and Lying Signs

You may have heard how to tell that a man is cheating, or maybe you can imagine what the signals might be. But I want to explore not only the signs that a husband *is* cheating, but also the signs that he is *about to cheat*. Here are the main clues you want to be acutely aware of.

Cheating Signals

"I read a book that gave me tons of signals that a man was cheating, but it was frankly overwhelming. When I spoke to my sister and dearest friends we all decided that so many applied to all of us, we didn't know what to believe." Robin was forty-seven and had two teenage daughters. Her husband was fifty-three and had recently bought a black convertible, started working out, ran his first marathon, and dyed his hair. Robin was convinced by the book she read that these were dead-on signals that her husband was cheating. But when she approached him he was emphatic that it was untrue. She didn't know what to believe. After all, she figured men do hit midlife and do some interesting things. Was it possible that her husband had decided to be healthier and enjoy life a bit more as part of his midlife crisis without cheating at the same time?

My research asked men to detail the warning signs they thought they gave their wives that hinted or told them they were close to an infidelity. I then asked them for warning signs that they were involved in infidelity. Both lists were quite similar, with only a couple of differences.

1. He Spends More Time away from Home

Fifty-five percent said more time spent away from home was a sign that they were close to infidelity, and it went up slightly to 61 percent when they were involved in infidelity. What's quite fascinating is that the majority of the men started spending more time away from home *before* they cheated. This warning sign and the ones below indicate not only that your husband *is* cheating but are also a precursor to his cheating. If you can catch the signs in time you might avoid the pain of infidelity and be able to repair your relationship. It's equally telling that during the affair 61 percent of the men spent more time away from home. Sometimes men will tell their wives to trust them because "I could cheat during my regular day if I wanted to." Although it's true that you can't possibly keep tabs on your husband's whereabouts during the workday, it still seems that cheating men find extra time to slip away from home, and not just during work hours. When you start to notice that your husband is spending less time at home, watch out and find out what's going on with him. It's worth discussing and trying to get him to articulate any dissatisfaction he may have in his life that causes him to want to spend less time at home or what new development has caused this sudden wanderlust. Remember, it's not proof that he's cheating, but it's pretty clear that he's close, and there should be no waiting on talking about changes to make your marriage better quickly.

Pepe told me he saw his mistress on his way home from work almost every day. She lived only a few blocks away so he could see her whenever he left the house. He'd go out on weekends to play softball and get there late after seeing the other woman. He'd offer to go grocery shopping for his wife so he could grab an extra half hour with his mistress. His wife never knew and still doesn't. "I was like a thief sneaking around. My wife never realized I was away as much as I was. I think we'd become so different anyway, our lives were somewhat different. She didn't want to watch me play softball and was happy if I'd leave to food shop." Pepe didn't think he was a great thief but felt his wife wasn't looking at the most obvious signal reported in the research. He was finding more and more excuses to be away from home. "Toward the end it got so ridiculous, like I wanted to get caught, that I told her I was going to play golf. I didn't even own clubs and she was just too distant at that point to ask what was going on."

2. You Have Sex Infrequently

The number two signal isn't surprising although the numbers are: thirty-four percent of men reported diminished sexual activity as a sign they were close to infidelity, and it rose 43 percent once the infidelity was under way. Again, it's noteworthy that 34 percent saw diminished sexual activity as a warning sign before any infidelity, telling you again that you can catch some of these signals before an affair or even unhappiness sets in. I did find it curious that only 43 percent said it was a signal of actual infidelity. You'd think there'd be a higher number if they're already having sex outside the marriage. It could be that they weren't having so much sex before, so it wasn't much of a change once the infidelity began.

Jorge highlighted this idea for me. I asked him how he could not have had any change in sex at home while he was cheating. He explained that he had sex about once every three weeks with his wife. When he was cheating, he still maintained the sex at home. "I didn't want to do that to my wife, but if we stopped having sex completely, she would've become suspicious. I didn't know what else to do."

Fifty-seven percent of cheating men will cheat and yet not have less sex with their wives, although the usual frequency could be once every couple of months in many struggling marriages. However, diminished sexual activity was still a large number, telling us that maintaining sexual consistency and frequency is essential for a healthy marriage.

3. He Avoids Contact with You

The next signal was "avoidance of contact (cell phone calls)," at 29 percent and dipping slightly to 24 percent once the infidelity began. The contact you have with your husband during the day, even if it is about the ordinary business of life, still helps you develop a general awareness of each other. His avoidance of your calls or desire not to spend time with you points to a desire to disconnect, whether he is conscious of it or not. Stay connected with little calls to say, "Hi, I love you" and "How is your day going?"

4. He Criticizes You More

"More criticism of wife" scored 25 percent but dipped to 19 percent once the infidelity began.

Stephanie didn't understand what was going on. "He used to love my cooking. My mother was Italian and he'd be proud of my ethnic dishes. All of a sudden, he was tired of my food and wanted me to 'mix it up' a bit. I was insulted but I tried other things and he seemed okay. But then he started on me for how I was spending the money. Ever since we were married I took care of the finances because I have an educational background in finance. Now he was questioning me and looking over my shoulder. Suddenly, he didn't like the way I was putting away our savings, and we had a huge fight over all of the changes he demanded." Six months later Stephanie discovered her husband was cheating and funneling money to help out his mistress.

5. He Starts More Fights with You

Twenty percent said they started more fights with their wives.

Notice that criticizing their wives and starting more fights can be seen as very similar signals. Put them together and you have a large portion of men who were more harassing to their wives.

Most cheating men spent more time away from home, avoided contact, and had less sex with their wives. These signals represented in changes in behaviors (and remember, they're only significant if there are *changes* in these areas) seem to indicate that the warning signals will be about your husband disconnecting from you. When you feel your husband has changed into a person who is disconnected from you, it's a sign of impending danger to your marriage.

Listen Closely—He May Tell You about the Other Woman

One final note is not something in my research, but a signal I've noticed many times in my work. Often, your husband will begin talking more and more about a woman, usually a colleague in the office or organizational board. He'll tell you they had lunch or ran into each other somewhere else and that her family went to such and such a place for vacation and her kids loved it. Your husband thinks you guys should go there for your next vacation. Since he hasn't had sex with her he's not hiding the relationship with her. But as he becomes friendlier you need to remember that most cheating occurs with friends, not one-night stands just for sex. So your husband might be telling you about his potential mistress straight to your face. He may even want you to meet her. Beware of admiring comments and begin to consider what needs to happen in your marriage so that your husband seems as excited to hear your ideas as those of his newfound friend. How does this woman seem to make him feel?

QUICK ACTION PROGRAM

Step Two: Change the Cheating Signals

We've discovered from cheating men the signals they give when they're getting ready to cheat. It's in your interest to be well acquainted with them and to take action as soon as you recognize any of them.

Ask yourself these five questions: if the answer is yes to any of them, consider what you can do to immediately change the circumstances.

1. Is my husband spending more time away from home?
   - What can I do to make him want to spend more time at home? (This is not to say it's all on you to fix the relationship. But you want to consider how the two of you can get along better at home so that it is a place he isn't beginning to avoid. Also consider the calmness of the home. If it is hectic with the children, consider how to change that and ask him to take a role in it.)
   - Discuss with him what he'd like to do along with you to make the home a happier place for both of you.

2. Are we having less sex?
   - Consider initiating more often.
   - Ask him for help with home duties so that both of you can create a calmer, happier atmosphere and have more energy for intimacy.

- Arrange for a night at a hotel without the children. Upon returning home, discuss how the two of you can add more lovemaking into your regular life.
- Consider what will add to your enjoyment of making love.

3. Is my husband avoiding my calls?
   - Consider if you're calling him about things that can be annoying for him to deal with during the day.
   - Ask him to commit to weekly time when you can sit with each other and discuss important issues that need to be resolved together.
   - Consider making calls just to remind him how much you love him and look forward to seeing him and making love.
   - Request that he call you with similar messages to those you've sent him.

4. Has my husband been more critical of me or started more fights with me?
   - Discuss with him how he can speak to you in such a way as to make suggestions without being critical.
   - Talk to him about complimenting you and how both of you can focus more on each other's positive traits.

Lying Signs

Jane's Story: A Wife and Two Lawyers

Jane was pregnant when she noticed the difference in her husband, who was a lawyer. They had shared a wonderful relationship in the first years of their marriage, but then things began to change. The changes were subtle for a long time, and frankly, Jane admitted that she rationalized all the signs away. After all, due to a complicated pregnancy, sex was difficult. She had con-vinced herself he was being thoughtful not to push the sex issue for many months. She didn't want to think anything of the cell phone that once lay on the dresser but now was always being recharged in the car.

She couldn't believe it when the words slipped out of her mouth during her ninth month. She remembered being more shocked than her husband when she asked, "Are you having an affair?" It was almost as if she had to say it without thinking, because to think and ponder it would be too painful. She was relieved when her husband not only denied it but was so taken aback that she knew it was an outrageous thought to him. "Are you kidding me? What could possibly tell you that?" He even went on to explain that he wanted to change whatever it was that was giving her doubts so that she would never have to live with that fear and concern. She continued with a sigh of relief as the conversation quickly turned light and chatty. She outlined the phone in the car, his lack of initiating sex, the times she couldn't reach him on his cell. He lovingly held her hand, explaining that he was in court much more these days and was unable to answer his phone, plus the phone often didn't work in the courthouse, but from then on he'd call her right back as soon as he was outside the courthouse. He explained that he thought sex was off the table and didn't want to bother her to "take care of him." He said he'd bring the phone in if it would make her feel better, but it was just so much easier to leave it in the car and never be interrupted with work calls at home.

Jane was so happy that she told him to leave his cell in the car and they worked out a cute signal for sexual con-tact, with no hard feelings if she wasn't up to it. "And I know now I was being silly and very hormonal," she said.

"Just call me whenever it's good for you. I don't want you
to feel any pressure through the day to have to look for
my missed call. Just get back to me now and then without
worrying about me when you're on your way to court or
something important like that."

Things changed a little after that. There was one time
he initiated sexual contact, and he did bring in his phone
a couple of nights. But the baby was soon crying at short
intervals throughout the night, and it wasn't until the baby
was four months old that Jane broached the subject again.
She knew she was overtired, stressed, and hormonal. But
she talked to her mother and they agreed something didn't
add up. Jane had received a cell phone bill that usually
went to her husband's office but was forwarded to the
home when there was a week's worth of renovation going
on at the office. A lot of mail had shown up that day, and
Jane later learned it was a mistake made by the new secre-
tary. Jane opened the bill and found out that her husband
had been in contact a great deal with someone at a number
she didn't recognize. She cried for hours until his return
home that evening, when she immediately confronted him.

"He was so cool and, if you can believe it, warm. He
laughed and said that he could understand how it looked
so bad but that it was a law office he'd been doing a lot of
business with lately. He explained that although he talked
to various lawyers there, he made calls through the switch-
board number since that was the one he had committed to
memory and he got connected to whomever he needed to
speak with. I called the number in front of him and sure
enough it was a major law firm in town. I felt like a fool."

Nevertheless, for the next five months Jane was beside
herself. She couldn't stop herself from wondering and
thinking about where her husband was and if he was

cheating or not. It was all-consuming to her, and finally when she began to bring up little inconsistencies, her husband stopped being Mr. Nice Guy and began getting angry at her for not letting it go. It was five months later that he told her he needed a separation to think things over and that it had nothing to do with anyone else. Jane didn't know what to believe anymore and begged him to finally speak the truth. But he remained firm in his protestations of fidelity, even citing her disbelief of him as one of the major reasons why he needed a break.

One Wednesday night, she met a former colleague of her husband at a charity dinner. "He told me that he was so sorry to hear about me and my husband but that I must be happy that at least it's all out and over. When I looked curiously at him, he realized he'd stuck his foot in his mouth. But he had no choice, and besides, it seemed like he felt bad for me." After a year, Jane finally heard the truth. Her husband had been cheating on her with a female colleague at the large firm he'd been calling so much. It seemed that everybody knew about it, and some people even assumed they were together at times. Jane was livid and, promising not to reveal the source of the information, contacted her husband.

"I just wanted the truth. I mean, he owed me that at the very least." Jane's husband flatly denied it all, explaining that he did know that woman and did have to work with her intensely on some cases, which may have been misinterpreted for something more. Today, he is living with the other woman and still claims that the relationship was never more than professional until after the separation.

Everyone knows lying is wrong, yet it seems almost everyone does it in some fashion. The lie "I'll call you" is so popular today that I think some have confused it as a substitute for "good-bye." Lying diminishes trust and distorts reality.

When we are lied to we can begin to feel like we're the crazy ones. We want to believe the ones we love; we want to depend on others to present the reality for us, because we are so reliant on our world being consistent and having a predictable outcome.

Naturally, you know that people, perhaps yourself, will lie if (a) you will be criticized if you tell the truth, or (b) you won't get caught. Still, we hope that those who love us—especially our children and spouse—will be honest even if doing so results in criticism and angry responses.

Why do cheating men lie? Prepare to be surprised. I've sat across from some fantastic liars who are not necessarily pathological—just really good liars who lie for understandable reasons. Men seem to believe that telling the truth about cheating is a really bad idea. They'll lie to their wives, marriage counselors, and parents.

There's a true story about a married man in court who denied even knowing a certain woman. The wife's attorney repeatedly grilled him, making sure the man testified that he had never seen the woman before in his life. It was only then that the attorney brought out multiple pictures taken by a private investigator of this man spending lots of time with the very woman he denied knowing. Satisfied, the attorney asked the husband how he could lie to the court. The man responded, "I didn't know you had the pictures."

This scenario seems to depict the typical cheating man—lie until you can't lie anymore. And then lie some more. Once a man tells the truth about cheating, life changes dramatically and with lightning speed. He loses, and losing doesn't come easy to any man. Plus, now he has to be more emotional. He'll have to be apologetic, feel true sadness for what he's done to you, feel like you now have the right to stick a video camera on his forehead to know his every move. So let's weigh the options for your husband. Lying seems to win out.

But what about love, you ask? What about his desire to truly connect and love you and get past this and grow from it even and work to make things better? Keep in mind that this man has cheated on you, which indicates some lack of love, a disconnect, feeling lost, and a dissatisfaction with you and the marriage. Emotional talk is not as comfortable for your husband as you might think. Like most men, he's been taught his whole life to be cognitive and logical. Under these conditions, lying wins out.

I'm quite fascinated by the distortion of reality and find it maddening for women I'm trying to help in my practice. Like Jane, these women become consumed by the need to know what's really going on. Once the lies begin, it's an excruciating road to ever trusting their husband again, assuming he finds a way to be honest. And there is no easy answer. The best I can give is that ultimately we trust our spouses because we feel connected enough in the relationship that we'd feel the slightest pulling away and can learn to reel things back in. Too often, couples just allow things to continue to disconnect and don't have a mechanism for reconnecting and making things better before they get out of hand. Even after cheating, this process is the ultimate healer. All the apologies in the world won't protect a marriage.

A *commitment to keep constant tabs on the relationship and doing what it takes to keep it working for both of you is the only answer.*

Do you think your husband would tell the truth if confronted about cheating? Let's see.

My research went to great lengths to pinpoint the percentage of cheating men who lied about the affair. (Turn to page 14 to compare the following stats with your guess.)

The results were scary. Fifty-five percent of cheating men have never told their wives about the affair, either because the wives have never asked or because they continued to lie about it even after their wives had evidence of the other relationship. Specifically, 28 percent never told and were never asked, while 27 percent lied even after their wives had some evidence of the relationship. Another 14 percent lied until their wives had evidence. Twelve percent told their wives after being questioned multiple times, 12 percent told after being questioned the first time, and a measly 7 percent told without being questioned. This means that only 31 percent told their wives because they were questioned.

Bottom line: if you're expecting your husband to be honest with you about his cheating—you'd better buy a lottery ticket. Too many wives have felt like they're being tortured when they sense something is up and are repeatedly convinced verbally from their husbands that they are way off. Being told to your face that your perceptions are completely wrong and rebelieving and trusting your husband's words when your heart and gut are telling you another story is absolutely tragic. There is no word to describe the experience of being lied to by the one person you chose to commit to for the rest of your life. And your husband has turned out to be a convincing liar, which just makes you think about how much you really don't know this man with whom you've shared everything, the most intimate parts of who you are, parts of yourself no one else may ever know.

Where Cheating Men Meet the Other Woman

Where does your husband pick up a new friend who could threaten your marriage? The number one place is the most obvious to me: work. Forty percent of the men in my research met the other woman at work. This suggests that you should keep very aware of who your husband is hanging out with at work. In my more than twenty years of helping couples, the identity of the mistress has rarely been a surprise to the wife when that mistress was met through work. That's often because the husband would speak of the other woman at some point, raising an eyebrow for the wife no doubt.

Listen carefully when your husband tells you that he and what's-her-name are working on a project together. The other woman's name will pop up from time to time and you should take that opportunity to seriously consider where your marriage is. That's the time not to delay any changes you've been wanting to make in your relationship.

Instead, you should go full throttle in doing so. And it probably requires an open conversation with your husband about the rules of your marriage. You don't have to jump all over him and make him recoil from your distrust. You only need to use what's-her-name as a catalyst for a clear discussion about what your husband will agree to do and not do—stay late for a meeting if it's only the two of them, travel together to conferences, have dinners out to discuss a project, and so on.

Beyond that, be aware not to talk a lot about how you and your husband are going to get closer. Just keep the conversation to agreeing on some rules for this new relationship. Then take heed and discover what you can do to create the kind of positive changes you've discussed with as little conversation as possible.

Thirty-two percent of the men met the other woman while engaging in some activity of personal interest. You might wonder if your husband has real passions that you have nothing to do with and ask yourself why. It could be because you have no interests in common (do I hear football?). But here's the deal. If your husband has a passion for something outside of you, what will happen when he meets another woman who shares that same passion? Sometimes as spouses we think we're being such good sports if we let our husbands spend time with their little-boy hobbies. But the men I interviewed are telling you that it's a mistake to let him roam freely in the world of his personal interests. If it's truly his time-consuming passion, be around now and then.

It's not enough to regularly send your husband off into a world you know nothing about and expect all of his energy around it to just stay still. He may look for someone else to connect with about it, and that may be the first step toward trouble. Realistically, I'm not suggesting that you become a sports fanatic. However, don't be so sure that you can't learn something about your husband's world that will at least allow you to talk with him about his interests. Should he always be going to professional sporting events without you because you just don't enjoy them? It depends on how many of these events he's going to. Consider these two factors:

- How often does this interest take him out of the house?
- How much does he discuss it with others?

For example, he watches football every Sunday at home with his two buddies while you pipe in now and then. Okay, he's home and he's not into it all week long, at least not beyond a comment here and there with his friends. Compare that with him going to a lot of games and having conversations throughout the week with buddies and listening to sports talk radio every chance he gets. He's found something he's passionate about and it absorbs a large part of him. Why wouldn't you want to get in on that? Why not learn about it so that you can connect to him about it all? Let him teach you and you'll spend quality time with him communicating with you about it. When you think about it that way, it sounds better than being forced to watch smelly men jump around and cheer at stupidity. If he keeps seeing another woman at the game and starts having fun discussions with her, even if he's already met a woman at work and can have a great time talking sports with her, there's a piece of him that you're missing. You can reel in that piece of him and enjoy the process of connecting even if it's about a topic that is uninteresting or silly to you.

Naturally, you'd like the same from him—a healthy desire to get involved with something that is of interest to you. And he should. You have a better chance of that if your marriage is one where you have shared your interests and moved in a direction to become involved in each other's interests. Taking the first step will add to your fun time with your husband and encourage him to do the same for you. Even if he doesn't reciprocate, you still gain the connection and protect your marriage more.

Seventeen percent of cheating men met the other woman in the neighborhood. Felipe was a cheater who met the other woman while they were doing charitable work together. "It was so pathetic how my wife kept pushing me into joining this neighborhood charitable group, thinking it would make me a better person, and that's where I met her. It was true that I almost always thought about money and needed to get some perspective, but being pushed into something like that wasn't going to work. My wife didn't come with me, because she had friends who insisted that she was always leading me too much and I needed to learn to do good things on my own without her help."

One last noteworthy piece of information regarding where these husbands met the other woman: only 3 percent reported meeting the mistress on the Internet. Keep in mind that about half of the men in the study responded to the questionnaire online, meaning they were capable Internet people. Still, although many cases could be made for how the Internet disrupts marriages, it does not appear to pose the biggest problem of your husband meeting someone online and having that lead to sex.

How Long Did It Take to Get from Meeting to Cheating?

Hal spoke candidly to me about his infidelity. "Julie and I had been boyfriend and girlfriend in college so when she moved back into town we got together at first to talk of old times. That was my first mistake. It was strange to think that the woman I was cheating with knew me longer than my own wife. I don't know why that meant so much to me, but it did. It still took me almost three years after her return before I cheated on my wife. So it must've been technically fifteen years that I knew her."

Here's the good news. The reason I talk about listening for the name of the new woman at work or at the ball game is that you will likely have some time to work on your marriage before anything awful happens. As much as you may worry about the one-night stand, only 6 percent of the cheating men had sex with a woman after meeting her the same day or night. Twenty-seven percent had sex within one month of meeting this other woman, which sounds very quick but will still give you some warning. But 36 percent of the men waited more than a month and up to a year before having sex. All told, 69 percent of the men said they had sex within one year of meeting the woman. It's scary to think how quickly things can deteriorate, but now that you're educated in what you can do about preventing it and how you can be aware of it before the worst strikes, consider yourself empowered to take the lead and create a solid marriage.

QUICK ACTION PROGRAM

Step Three: Get Involved in His Work and Play Lives

Seventy-two percent of cheating men met the other woman either at work or through an activity of personal interest, so learn as much as you can about these two areas of your husband's life. They represent major parts of who he is, and he puts enormous energy into both. Become a part of that energy.

1. Get involved in his work.
   - Have daily chats about what went on.
   - Show genuine interest in details about his day. There's an old saying, "If you want better answers, ask better questions." Find out some details about his work (projects, deadlines) and also ask about office politics and gossip. This will help you know his surroundings at work and give you an emotional sense of it.

2. Get involved in his hobbies.
   - Familiarize yourself with his interests so that he can converse with you about them. Otherwise he will keep all of that positive energy for others.

- Become a part of it. You don't have to demand that he never watch another ball game, go jogging, or attend charitable organization meetings without you. But there is no reason why you wouldn't want to play a more active role by being present more than you have been. Perhaps if you open yourself to his hobby, you will feed off his energy and you'll have a collective interest that can only increase your friendship.

Why You Want to Know ASAP if Your Husband Is Cheating

There is a severely complicated issue around lying that many people miss. Usually, as my research shows, there is lying and it continues for a period of time. It's during this time that the ability to ever repair the relationship diminishes. Cheating is more than the cheating itself. It's also about the lying. A man who tells his wife about the cheating without putting her through months of painstaking torturous confusion trying to figure out what's going on is a man who has a better chance of repairing his relationship. For every lie that is avoided, there is a greater chance of success, because it is the lying that causes wives to feel as though they can never trust their husband again.

Just cheating is bad enough. But if a man finds himself lost and comes to his wife and says "I (or we) need help" after his wife has been lied to straight into her eyes, she has the unfortunate task of not only getting over the affair but also figuring out whether she and her husband can repair their marriage. She worries about whether she will trust that he won't cheat again and lie over and over about it.

If a husband hasn't lied to his wife and they're able to work things out, she'll be able to trust that if she ever asks him when she finds him pushing the marital boundaries in any way, he'll be honest with her. Believe it or not, that can make all the difference in whether a wife will ever feel good about her marriage again.

Unfortunately, if your husband has cheated there's a 93 percent chance he's not going to tell you (and an 81 percent chance he won't tell you even after you initially question him). If your idea is to keep badgering him about it until he cracks, guess what? Bad, bad idea. The longer you continue that process of feeling that something is going on and waiting for him to come clean while he continues to lie to you, the farther away you are from being able to repair your marriage.

If you feel he is cheating and he denies it, take action—check cell phone bills and e-mails, ask friends or relatives you can trust if they've heard anything suspicious, or hire a private investigator—for your sake and for the sake of your marriage.

4

Understanding the Male Mind: Connecting Emotionally

Think of an eleven-year-old boy playing in a football league. His team loses on the last second of the game because he made a mistake. The other team and parents are cheering, his teammates are strewn over the field on their backs and knees, and this boy is holding his head in his hands, afraid to see what it looks like to let down his team at the most important point of the year. His dad walks over to him and puts his hand on his back and says something like, "You played hard," and then notices his son tearing up. Dad follows up his comment with a gruff, grunting whisper of "Keep it together. Wait until you get in the car."

The scene is pretty typical. Most boys are involved in some sort of competition, usually sports, and if not, chess or spelling bees. Competition brings highs and lows. And boys learn all along how to be good winners and losers. But winning is key. Some parents are more involved than others and some will be softer than others. And in today's world many fathers have learned a softer, more accepting approach, to a point. But the bottom line is, no matter how far we've come in our modernized society, boys are taught early on to withhold emotions and control them. They are forced to compartmentalize so that they can get out on the field, court, or ice for the next play and still be a winner, ignoring any pain endured from the play before. Their idols are the sports heroes who only take off a day when a parent passes and then play the next game, intending to win it for the deceased parent. No one likes a crybaby. If the hero's wife has a baby, today's sports world has changed to allow for a sports celebrity to actually leave the team to be there for the birth, but hey, you'd better be back—sweet, loving Daddy—and ready to crush some bones in the game a couple of days later. If a boy is too "feeling," he risks being called a sissy.

Men have to be as tough as nails and constantly able to put aside their feelings. That's what wins wars, builds companies, and makes the manly world go 'round. Or at least that's what we've all learned as boys. A wife needs a trainer? Get out there and exercise, he says. A wife is afraid of something? Suck it up. A wife is sad because her best friend has breast cancer? Okay, but what can she do to resolve the issue? What? You want your husband to feel bad about it, to just slow down and feel what it's like to be given such news?

Many women find it hard to believe that their husbands can't understand the simplest sad emotions. They take it quite personally when their husbands can't spare the time to offer loving support, caring responses, and truly share in their wives' emotions. I'm not saying they can't, nor am I saying you should give up hope. I'm merely saying that for most men, the starting point is farther away than you would have expected.

But He Used to Be More Sensitive

Sure, your husband may have been different when you were dating him. You might say that he knows how to be so wonderfully caring because he did it before or else you never would've married him. But this fits into his winning attitude. When he was dating you, he was on a mission and was able to do whatever it took to win, to get you to truly love him and marry him. But once you married, there were new goals to win—having a family, owning a house, building a better career—and those goals easily became the focus of the new winning attitude.

Nicole spoke to me about how much her husband had changed. "Rick was unbelievably attentive and sensitive before we got married. All of my girlfriends would call and talk to him because he was the guy who understood them and could give them a sensitive guy's view. On my birthday two months before we got married, he arranged for the chef of my favorite restaurant to cook an unbelievable dinner that was served on a private area of a beach where the restaurant specially set up a table and the whole dinner. When we were moving into our new house, he had arranged for a carpenter to create a special shoe organizer in my closet. I thought I was home free. But then, soon after we were married, Rick went out on his own and started his advertising firm. All of a sudden I felt like all of the attention to detail on me was going to his clients."

Nicole watched in disbelief as Rick hired the same chef that provided her birthday dinner to cater an over-the-top holiday party on a rented yacht. Her husband would spend every spare moment taking her shopping for the finest cigars, the unusual brands his clients preferred, while having no energy to find the hard-to-get Birkin bag that he had promised for their upcoming anniversary. "It wasn't that I didn't understand how much energy he had to put into his work. It was just so odd the way it seemed like the attentiveness and sensitivity to me was completely lost and refocused on his clients. I know I'm not crazy. If I'd tell someone new this story, she'd say that I should have seen it coming. But it really wasn't a 'love is blind' thing. He really was so different before we married. He really is the same caring guy, it's just that somehow it's no longer focused on me."

Yes, your husband has a lot of emotion in him. But he has been taught repeatedly to think instead of feel and to put emotions on the back burner. So he hasn't had the experience you wish he'd had in being aware of and verbalizing his emotions. At the same time that he was taught to keep emotions at bay, he was taught to do anything for a teammate, to feel brotherhood and risk anything because of the ties he'd be expected to develop and feel for his teammates. This is why so many men present a very complex picture. They are obviously emotional, and women pick up on it, but then the men are not emotional in the areas that it seems they should be. Women have little choice but to take it personally.

The good news is that men do love. They desperately want to love and be loved, and this is the key that allows great marriages to happen. But the greater the knowledge you have of your husband's emotional process, the better you will be at bringing out the very best emotional part of him.

The Number One Mistake Wives Make: If I Appreciate Him, He'll Never Change

I've counseled enough women to know that some are concerned that if they are appreciative, their husbands might get the wrong impression and think they no longer need to work any harder at anything. This line of thinking will not accomplish your goal. Cheating men might have perhaps had wives who didn't want to risk too much appreciation in the hope that their voicing dissatisfaction would motivate change in their husbands.

Men are motivated by appreciation. They don't sit there and say, "Great, I got her where I want her. She thinks I'm fantastic, so I can stop trying to please her or working harder at making more money." They know the bills might be growing next year. They haven't forgotten that you'd like them to spend more time with you and less time playing poker online. Appreciation is not going to invite your husband to reduce his physical or emotional efforts to be a man. It will only cause greater warmth between the two of you and fuel his desire to make you happy.

Miguel watched his children one night while his wife went out with friends for a "girls' night out." It wasn't easy for him as his four-year-old ended up vomiting more than once and Miguel did his best to keep things clean and calm.

"Then the following night I wanted to invite a couple of buddies over to watch the World Cup and my wife refused because we were supposed to see her parents, who live in town for half the year. I told her that I watched the kids last night, and that should account for something. She told me that they're my kids too so why should I expect points for taking care of my own kids? I know she made sense, but I was so frustrated. After we got into a huge fight she told me that if she let me watch then I'd expect to watch all of the World Cup with my friends for weeks. Come on. I knew I wasn't some teenager. I knew I had responsibilities. It really bothered me because it was like she was telling me that she had married some jerk. I did too many nice things to be told I can't do something because then I'll do it all the time."

Miguel spoke to me like many men who felt their wives had an ulterior motive for withholding appreciative comments and gestures. They felt belittled and controlled by the thought of their wives not wanting to be too nice because it might cause their husbands to stop doing what their wives wanted them to.

Why Do I Have to Appreciate Him to Get Him to Be Good to Me?

Women often have an issue wrapping their minds around the idea that their husband will be good to them only if they know they're going to get something out of it. "I want a man who loves me unconditionally and just wants to be around me and love me just because I'm me."

That's an understandable premise but it really speaks to the idea of being fully loved well beyond what you can do for your husband.

All of us want to feel completely accepted, but that's more fairy tale than reality. The reality of life is that we are judged and develop our relationships based on what we bring to them. Only a parent can feel that ultimate love and acceptance even if that child seemingly "does" nothing for the parent. But keep in mind that your kid is a genuine part of you, so even if she doesn't do anything you still love her because she's an extension of you. Her success is your success.

Giving your husband what he wants doesn't reduce his love for you or desire to please you at all. It doesn't mean that he'll only be nice to you this week if you are nice to him. It doesn't mean he won't be by your bedside if, God forbid, you're hospitalized for a month and can't give him what he'd like. The more appreciative gestures you offer him, the more likely he is to feel great about giving you what you want. That's true love—learning to bring out the best in the one we love with our own effort.

Rachel's Story: A Healing Vacation

Rachel was irate at first when her husband floated his vacation plans. He traveled incessantly for work and when he was in town he worked late most nights at the office. So when he had a week of vacation coming his way, his idea of Rachel joining him for a half-week mountain-biking tour seemed preposterous. "I mean, he never gets to see the kids enough and his one week off he decides to spend half of it away from his kids? I understood he needed to work off steam and unwind, but your kids need you." Then Rachel spoke to her mother, who surprisingly told her to go on the trip with her husband and she'd stay with the kids. "I couldn't believe it. I thought for sure my mother would be as upset as I was, but she really seemed to feel that it was kind of a good thing that my husband wanted to go away with me alone, so I did it. I work too, but I'm more of a spa person. I had to take a week off of work as well, and the last thing I wanted to do was go traipsing around a mountain with a group of overachieving exercisers.

"Well, it was the smartest thing I ever did. First of all, he was so appreciative that he was the nicest he'd ever been while on the trip, so concerned that I was having a good time. On the trip he admitted that he never in a million years thought I'd ever say yes. He gave me a chance to talk about how much we missed him at home and how much the kids needed him. He really listened for the first time and we returned with a weekend plan that included family time and he really came through. I mean, I could always want more, but it was a big improvement and really the first time I felt we were working together as a team when it came to the kids."

Rachel learned firsthand that thoughtful, appreciative gestures go a long way to connecting to your husband. Most often that appreciation does not cause your husband to ignore your desires, it motivates him to want to please you more. If you want his attention, start with loving appreciation.

Find His Goodness

How does a wife appreciate? The same way a husband does: in the ways your spouse *wants* to be appreciated. You might want flowers, jewelry, a verbal compliment, breakfast in bed. What does your husband want? Consider your man. He wants you to appreciate him with gestures that are meaningful to him. Letting him get away without cleaning up one night because he's had a big day, giving him some space to watch the game, telling him how he turns you on. What would he say are the things you could tell him and do to show him he's appreciated?

Unfortunately, he's not going to tell you with such clarity. Yes, he might grope you, blurt out in a mumble that he never gets time to watch the game, and so on. But he's not going to lovingly hold your hand and say, "I love it when you appreciate my hard work by making time for us to make love." Verbalizing with such simple clarity is not his forte. It's up to you to consider what would be meaningful forms of appreciation for him.

There was another message the cheating men shared. They weren't looking for their wives to appreciate them so much. They just felt that their wives' appreciation and thoughtful gestures had slowed to an eventual grinding halt and they were left with the feeling that they did little or nothing right anymore.

Your job isn't to turn into an appreciation machine, just to continue adding to your loving gestures. Accomplish this one and the odds of him ever cheating on you really go down.

Cynthia's appreciative gesture was creative, so it stuck out in my mind. She videoed herself singing "their" song and put it on YouTube with an appreciative message at the end. One night when her husband was working on his computer she interrupted him and took him to it. "He went wild, and before I knew it his friends were telling him how much they wished their wives would be so nice and appreciative. I got a lot of points with that one and he can watch it over and over and keep hearing how much I love him and am thankful that I have him."

Appreciating Your Husband

List ways you think your husband would want you to show him your appreciation:

How can I show appreciation verbally?

How can I show appreciation physically?

How can I show appreciation through warm and thoughtful gestures?

The Three Keys to Understanding Your Man

1. Winning Is Everything

Men are commonly not interested in fighting a losing battle. They are trained to find the winning edge, and if they can't win as a team then at least they have to win as an individual. Have you seen men watch professional sports? Have you seen their mood change depending on the outcome of the game they watch or participate in? Many men in this research spoke to this winning attitude as it related to their marriages with very common phrases like, "I felt I couldn't win no matter what I did." When a husband feels that his wife is so upset with him that he can't really win anymore, he immediately compartmentalizes his feelings toward her. This in turn causes her to feel angrier at him because he's becoming more emotionally distant, which causes him to try less and less because his wife is always so angry at him. The wife has been on his case because she feels she needs him to make a real change and doesn't want him to believe that one nice act is going to wash away all of the other insensitive stuff he did. So even after he does something nice she's careful not to give him too much in the win column for fear he'll think everything's fine, all back to normal, and he'll stop trying. This was a really common scenario these men spoke to, and it's a failed system.

One husband in my research claimed that every time he came home after work he was greeted by a sour look on his wife's face. She was upset at him on a daily basis for anything and everything. It didn't take too long before he didn't want to come home anymore. He admitted to being difficult to live with but still felt he was a solid father and was working very hard to support the family. On the one hand, he knew he could be much better. He understood his wife's complaints. But on the other hand, he felt he wasn't as horrible as his wife made him feel.

"I mean, it was like there was nothing about me she liked. Why was I going to change one bit for her? I just couldn't win."

After a while it just became easy for him to find intimacy with his wife's friend, who was also unhappily married.

"We had a lot more in common, and of course it was wrong, but she liked me. Yeah, I knew she'd probably think differently if she lived with me, but it just felt too good."

His wife shared with me that she was angry and felt that simply accepting him wasn't good enough. She decided she wasn't going to stay with him unless he made changes in his ability to be emotionally connected to her. But what she came to understand through incredible pain was that her always being critical and upset with him was never going to let him win at any stage and therefore could never motivate him to bring out the best emotional person he could be.

Phil's Story: A Winning Scenario

"I haven't cheated, but I came close," Phil began his story during our interview. "I had been getting too friendly with someone at work, and basically we had to travel together to a conference and it would've gone too far. But this, I don't know, maybe divine intervention, put some moments together that saved me. A few days before I traveled my wife and I went out with some of my friends on a Saturday night. They were some younger guys from work, mostly single. My wife and I were married fourteen years at the time, and it was different being with these younger guys and hearing what they were talking about. When we got home, my wife looked at me and told me that she still remembered why she married me that night. She said that being with those young guys showed her how much of a gem I was and how happy she was to have spent her youth with me. Looking at those guys just made her say the nicest things to me.

Then the next workday she had a single yellow rose sent to my office for me. When we were young, she loved yellow roses and I often sent dozens of them to her office back then. It had a note with similar things she had said on Saturday. It was really meaningful, and frankly, it was the difference between me going overboard with the woman I had gotten too close to. The trip was on Wednesday and went through the weekend. I really backed off from this other woman and she was shocked, but I explained to her I had made some mistakes letting the friendship go as far as it had. She was of course much younger, and I had lost my head a little. But my wife reminded me just at the right moment that it wasn't worth it. I never asked my wife if she did it because she felt I was drifting away or not, but whatever the case, it still made a lasting impression."

So it doesn't serve you well to say nothing and make no positive acknowledgment when he calls to tell you he'll be late for dinner after you yelled at him for the fifth time last week when he left you with a cold roast and no phone call. I know you feel and perhaps you are correct that he should not "get anything" or be appreciated for common courtesy. But if his effort fails to get any recognition—whether it's a quick thank-you or, much better, a really nice hug when he does return home—he hasn't won and there's little motivation in his male mind to continue on that path. Men don't actually think in terms of winning with their wives. But they do think things like, "What good was that? I called ahead like she wanted and she's still upset about something."

The men in my research taught me very clearly that when a man can't win at home, he'll start looking to win somewhere else.

Some men told me that their wives were so suspicious of their cheating that they finally did cheat. I responded with the obvious, "But if you ended up cheating, doesn't that really prove in retrospect that your wife was right to be suspicious?" They had no clear answer, but they told me that they felt that if their wives were not constantly trying to catch them they would not have cheated. They were thinking, "Why go to lengths to avoid cheating if my wife is going to think I'm cheating anyway?" It's a simple lose-lose concept to these men. If they can't win at home, it's time to find a new game they can win at.

The opposite is also true. When men feel like they can win at home, they'll go to the nth degree to please their wives. So learning to offer up appreciation and loving gestures will get you a husband who will continue to work at being more sensitive and emotional with you. He'll work very hard at being a winner at his marriage and family if you can lead the winning way. When he feels he's gaining ground he will continue to make a sincere effort to return your love consistently.

2. Men Compartmentalize

Men find it hard to understand why their wives can't hold on to their emotions and deal with them at a later time. Wives don't like it that their husbands can't take a moment or two to talk to them about their issues on the phone. "All it would take is a simple understanding comment and I'd be on my way," you might think. You could be right, but your husband doesn't think or speak on those levels as easily as you do. So if you have a car accident, it would likely be easy for him to say, "Oh my gosh, are you hurt, are you okay?" You might get a "You must be so shaken up." But when you call because you're upset that your five-year-old son wasn't watched properly on the playground and he got hit with a branch by another kid and it made a small cut right below his eye but one centimeter closer and he could've been blinded, he's not sure why he has to deal with this now.

You're upset and angry? Okay. If your kid is okay then there's no emergency. Your emergency is your justifiably angry, protective emotions. The likelihood is that women who are working outside the home might stop their day faster, talk to the nanny, leave work earlier than a man would. But your husband thinks it can wait. His asking you to wait and hold on to those emotions isn't his idea of being insensitive of you. It's what he'd ask of himself. If he got the call and found out the same information, chances are he would go on about his workday and file it all later to remind himself that he'd better call the principal and give him a piece of his mind. Unfortunately, he doesn't tell you this and possibly just ignores your feelings, thinking, "If the kid's okay, go on with your day and we'll figure it out later." If you continue to talk about it and even imply that he's being insensitive to you for not taking time out of his day to calm and soothe you, you risk him telling you that you're being insensitive for not respecting what kind of day he's having at work that you want to deal with it all now.

Henry's Story: Finding a Compromise

Henry and his wife both worked in the legal field but for different firms and areas of the law. "She was having some real backstabbing going on at her workplace and of course I felt bad for her, but hey, work sucks a lot of the time. She'd call me, and any advice I'd give, primarily to just be quiet and take it, got her angry. So she went and did what she wanted, and as soon as she told her boss's boss, the entire office politics exploded and she was being treated like crap. Okay, I understand. But she'd call me at work still complaining about it all.

"And I'm thinking, 'If you'd listened to me, you wouldn't be in this situation. Why do I have to listen to your complaining?' She never acknowledged that my suggestions in the end were the right ones. Her entering the workforce and seeing how difficult it was didn't seem to make her any more appreciative toward me for what I had to put up with. Then she wanted to quit, which would have meant a huge hit to our financial goals. I really got angry.

I just didn't want to hear it anymore and explained that I didn't want her to call me at work, period, and that I was done listening to all of this." Soon after that Henry's wife found her own emotional support from an online working mothers' support group. It wasn't long before each of them was doing their own thing.

"She went on the computer a lot for her support and I watched a lot more TV. We pretty much stopped going out and having sex, and it was largely over in my mind."

You want to find a compromise now that you understand more about how your husband works. If he can't help you with your feelings right now, learn together to commit to dealing with those issues at a later time, in the evening, for example. You may be concerned that he'll never want to deal with any feelings later, but he will if he feels he can win. At the same time you can ask him to just tell you that he's really busy and feels bad for you but would like it if you guys could wait until tonight to discuss it, so that you can get a momentary commitment to have him hear your feelings and he can get on with his day.

3. Men Don't Like to Complicate Things

Men have been trained to solve a problem and get on with it. Otherwise they're not quite sure what they're supposed to do. If you share an issue with your husband, the most likely response will be something along the lines of, "Well, why don't you just _____." He doesn't know that you're not yet interested in a solution but rather just want some understanding. He's been taught forever not to acknowledge his own emotions and not to expect others to rally around him and feel along with him. This is why he'll likely be resistant to your verbalizing emotional support to him.

He doesn't want to hear you say in a soft voice, "I feel so bad for you that your boss embarrassed you in front of your colleagues and made you feel little." He wants to be a winner and he wants you to understand, not through sensitive remarks but through emotional love. He wants you to be especially kind to him that night and make him feel like his idiot boss is a loser and he is a winner because he goes home at night and has a wife who loves him and wants to make love to him.

Since your husband isn't looking for the same type of feeling, sensitive comments when he's upset, he doesn't get it so clearly that you want words of encouragement, love, and support when you are sharing your daily struggles or accomplishments. He loves you and wants to make you happy, but this isn't going to register to him as an initial response. So you might have to clue him in to what you want—many times—because it's not his instinctual response in his own world of winning man. His world is about simplicity.

"You hurt, kid? No? Then get the hell out there and play. What? Your shoulder hurts? You got another shoulder, use it." He'd love to love you in the way you'd like, because deep down he seeks as much of an emotional connection as you do. He's just been trained to manage emotions very differently.

How to Show Him Support

Consider how you can show him supportive, loving gestures. First of all, when he tells you a story about someone who he felt wronged him, take his side immediately. Let him know you think the other person is wrong, disgusting, and inappropriate if any of that is true. This is really no different from what you want him to do for you. You may want it in a loving, soft voice and he may want it in a more matter-of-fact voice, meeting his tone. Be careful not to use motherly gestures when he's sharing a problem ("Aw, honey, that wasn't nice"). Rather, speak to his masculine side. Think about how his best male friend would respond and get as close to that as you feel comfortable ("Your boss is such an idiot. Of course you're pissed"). Have your emotion match his own. If he's angry, allow yourself to get a little hot and show him you're angry for him. If he's delighted, smile broadly and let him know he deserves it ("Unbelievable, you must be flying high. You deserved it after everything you've done over there").

Again, don't turn into a mother ("Wow, I'm so proud of you"). You can make motherly statements later when they are attached to a supportive gesture or written on a card, but they are not what he wants at the moment of sharing. Later on you can ask him if perhaps the other person said what he said because he misunderstood the situation. You can try to help your husband find another way to look at it. But this should come, if at all, at a quiet time later. If offered at the time he's sharing his feelings with you, he'll see you as unsupportive and taking the other team's side, and he will not want to be on your team.

A kind shoulder, back, or foot rub is a physical gesture that says, "Thank you for sharing. I understand you can use a little extra warmth and I'm just the person to give it, so keep on sharing with me." Cooking or arranging a meal and setting up a fun time out are simple and much-appreciated gestures. Sex is another wonderful gesture because it isn't condescending and always makes him feel wanted and accepted. It says, "I don't care what the hell the world is giving you out there, here at home you're the greatest and deserve my love. I always want to be close to you." All of these examples of supportive gestures serve as a great counterbalance to the messages he receives from the outside world that he might be complaining about. This is the way to keep your husband discussing his issues with you on a regular basis and keeping him on your team.

How to Clue Him In

We know men are different from women. Too often you assume your husband knows how to reach you and connect on a regular basis. Like many marital skills, it takes time and repetition to learn

---

The Three Keys to Understanding Your Man

1. Winning is everything: Make sure he feels he can win you over. Show him that even with his flaws and mistakes you see his best qualities and love that about him.

2. Men compartmentalize: Avoid emotionally complicated calls in the middle of his workday. Set up a successful scenario for him to hear you—a quiet, relaxed time when you're both well fed.

3. Men don't like to complicate things: They like to give answers and move on. Clue him in as to what you want, an understanding supportive response with interested follow-up questions—time for him to listen and get to know you. Let him know you don't want him to judge your feelings. He needn't agree or disagree, only try to feel what you're experiencing.

---

your spouse's unique habits and preferences. Unfortunately, we tend to spell out what we want only after we're frustrated because we aren't getting it. By that time our spouse feels attacked and misses our points. Consider it pleasant conversation to teach your spouse how he can win you over and stay deeply connected to you. Here are ten tips to help you.

1. You need to help him understand what it is you're looking for. It's likely you will have to draw him a map.
2. You don't want his quick advice, so you'll have to express this to him. Explain that you're very interested in his advice but that is not what you're looking for when you first share anything with him. Advice can come later.
3. You want him to understand you. Ask him to lose himself, to not think anything about himself for the moment and just consider, "How does my wife feel in this situation that she's sharing?"

4. Tell him that if he *understands* your feeling, it does not necessarily follow that he has to agree with you. A man is terrified of this concept. He thinks that if he understands how you feel when he gets home late from work, it means he'll have to stop working late. This is not true. He can be sensitive to your dilemma and still explain why he must work late. Hopefully, his understanding you will help him creatively compromise so that both of you feel you've made gestures that have considered each other's point of view.

5. Give him some concrete examples of what you'd like to hear him say in response to your sharing personal issues: "I understand how angry/sad/thrilled/nervous you are." He needs to know that he doesn't have to say a lot but be a good listener by offering comments that say he's getting you.

6. Let him know that he shouldn't glance at his BlackBerry or at the TV for a quick update on the day's scores when you're in the midst of sharing with him.

7. Give him the words "Tell me more" as a way of saying something that lets you know he's interested. Tell him to ask follow-up questions that give you the opportunity to give more information about the thoughts and feelings you're sharing.

8. You may want a hug at the moment that you're discussing a difficult issue. Make sure you tell him that as a general rule he should approach you with a hug and gentle gestures. Don't assume he knows this about you, because he probably does *not* want an empathic, sweet hug when he's sharing with you about his lousy day.

9. Tell him not to make a wisecrack about a roll in the hay at the moment you're sharing your stuff, even if that would be what he would want if the circumstances were reversed.

10. Some women don't like offering this clarity for their husbands, feeling that it takes away the spontaneity and is not as special unless he comes to figure these things out on his own. Try to

see past this. He likely just doesn't know what you're looking for. And for most men, knowing what to do to satisfy their wives' needs is so foreign to them that their wives need to repeat these messages over time. He does want to please you and feel that he has won you over.

Ann's Story: Family Issues

Ann had just about had it with her older sister. As usual, even though Ann was kind enough to make her sister incredibly comfortable when she visited, the sentiment was never returned when Ann visited her sister. Because Ann was much wealthier than her sister, she paid for her sister's trips and went to much trouble to make her feel like she was staying at the Ritz. But on the most recent visit, not only did her sister fail to make the room Ann stayed in nice, but she had also made "plans she absolutely couldn't break" two out of the four nights Ann was visiting. This sister was Ann's only close relative as her parents and one younger brother had already passed away.

"When I shared this with my husband, Gerald, all I wanted was for him to understand and help me figure out a way to discuss this with my sister. He makes a living negotiating deals, so if anyone could help me navigate the conversation, it would be him. Instead, in a cavalier manner, he told me to never visit her again and for me to stop complaining about it. He then told me he would refuse to go to my sister's son's wedding that year because of how she'd treated me. It was as if it was so much easier for him to just dispense this short, simple advice with no regard for my feelings."

Ann had many valid points, of course. But was her husband unsympathetic? His version was that he had done exactly what he thought

Ann wanted him to. He had solved her problem. He claimed to be so upset for her that he just wanted to protect her by stopping these painful feelings from occurring again. He missed the boat big time, but it wasn't because he didn't care.

Finding the Time to Love Each Other

Too often I've heard marital experts go to such lengths to teach detailed "skill building" that the whole process seems doomed to fail from the start. Not many of us want to go back to school in order to learn how to get along with our husband. And I don't believe that couples today have suddenly lost the ability to talk properly. Rather, our society today has lost the peace.

The best way I can describe what I mean is through a conversation I once had with my aunt Sylvia, married forty-five years and still talking of marriage in a warm wonderful kind of way. She explained to me that when she first married, she and my uncle couldn't afford a home phone. She claimed this was not unusual for the day. So for the entire first year of marriage, each came home from their job and schooling and were home, alone, with each other, with no interruption, not even a phone. It almost sounds like an alternate reality to me. But something occurred to me. I don't think they were particularly more skilled at marriage than most people today, they just had what few of us have now: uninterrupted time together. Somewhere between our BlackBerries (my wife calls mine my "CrackBerry," claiming she read a study that equated the brain waves of BlackBerry users with those of crack addicts), cell phones, e-mails, and computers, we're supposed to fit in a little marital time here and there. Life used to be challenging just because we had to manage kids, bills, and social calendars. Now the world is at our fingertips and it's put our spouses at arm's length.

It's quite fascinating that if I were to ask you what it takes to be a great parent or a great career woman, you'd immediately tell me things like "hard work, tremendous effort, intense focus." But if I asked you what it would take for you to be a great wife, you'd likely scratch your head a bit and wonder out loud, "Well, we went on vacation sometime in the last millennium. We had lunch out recently . . . oh wait, that wasn't lunch, it was a funeral." It seems that all of us want to ignore in our marriage the primary principles for success for every other part of our lives and somehow expect a glorious outcome. Don't bet on it. In order for you to cultivate intimacy and appreciation into the relationship, it'll likely take more focus and time together. Many couples tell me that they're great on vacation, but that's not the real world. What they don't realize they're saying is that they've found the answer to their problems but don't know how to infuse it into everyday living. They don't need a weekend seminar to teach them how to say "I feel" instead of "Your lousy mother told me . . ." although I think marital seminars can only help. What you likely need is an attitude that forces you to take uninterrupted time to sit in the peacefulness of your union. Time to talk, watch something funny on TV, cook or clean together, read side by side.

According to Cecile Andrews in her book *The Circle of Simplicity,* the average American couple spends only twelve minutes a day talking. Great, a whole lot of appreciating going on there. Interestingly enough, according to Andrews the average American spends six hours a week shopping. I ask every couple I help to spend at minimum four forty-five-minute periods a week of uninterrupted time together. This is not time that has to be filled with verbal conversation. Quite the opposite. Most men really don't want to be engaged, especially in "emotional" discussions about how their marriage is doing. Just shoot them now and get it over with. You don't have to talk about deep emotional issues in order to improve your marriage. You just have to create enough space for the two of you to let nature do what it did to get you together in the first place. Have fun, talk politics, complain about your clergyperson (I'm a rabbi, I can say that). Anything that you do together even while in your own home will make you feel like a couple again, and that focus will help you do loving things automatically.

Another basic way to help the emotional side of your relationship is the date night. You've probably heard the concept before. My prescription is for a weekly date night, a minimum of two hours alone. Don't invite another couple or your depressed brother to tag along. People can meet you after the two hours on that night to continue your time if you'd like. You can talk about anything except three subjects: kids, money, and business. I know you're probably thinking what everyone tells me: "What else are we ever going to talk about? This is all we ever discuss." Remember when you were dating? Talk about the stuff you talked about then. Prepare a little for the date. Do something interesting and fun. Do a Web search for some funny sites. The point is, I'm pretty sure you were not talking incessantly about the stress of money, kids, and business when you were dating, because if you were, you never would've gotten married. That kind of conversation didn't make you fall in love. I don't know why you think it's going to sustain your love.

"It was like the last thing I wanted to do," Frank said, referring to his wife's idea of dating fun. "But I had cheated a year before and one of my promises to my wife when we worked it out was to try new things and spend more time together. I thought we could just go to the movies and dinner. When she told me she signed us up for salsa-dancing lessons, I wanted to scream. But it turned out to be the best thing. It was fun doing something we both had never done before and weren't very good at. As time went on, not only did we enjoy it but it opened a window where we started going out more to other clubs where we could dance. All of sudden we had something in common that we really enjoyed, and dancing keeps you pretty close and sensual. Plus, the other couples in the group were people who wanted to spend time together in their marriage, so I moved away from all of those friends who always complained about their wives and girlfriends and found some guys who, like me, enjoyed being with their wives. We really started to relate and enjoy each other in a way we never had and I never thought we could."

Obviously you need time to talk about the stresses of life, and it works much better when you identify a time to do that so that those topics don't bleed over into every other part of your relationship like some uncared-for wound. Imagine if you had one time for one hour where you talked about the business of life—let's say every Saturday or Sunday morning—and then you could move on with your day and focus on other things. It wouldn't mean that you could not discuss stressful items as they came up in the week, but it would go a long way toward stopping indiscriminate pressure-filled conversations that suck the energy out of your relationship. It's crucial that your marriage doesn't turn into managing a business, and that's why anything you can do to lead the way to kindness and appreciation will land you a significantly happier, safer marriage that will send wonderful things back to you as well.

The Role of Guilt

Another major aspect of a man's psychology is guilt. Does he feel the least bit guilty? Does guilt mount, diminish, or ever have a place in the cheating man's heart?

"I guess you feel guilty at first, but you kind of explain it to yourself," said Craig, age forty-one, a father of two, who is still married. "It gets so crazy that I actually said to myself my wife wouldn't mind deep down because this way I won't be bothering her for sex or attention so much anymore. You become so good at rationalizing it that when my wife would get mad at me I'd think, 'No problem, Suzy [the other woman] likes me the way I am,' and would use it as an excuse to go to her."

Most cheating men feel guilty, but guilt will not stop a husband from cheating. Two-thirds of cheating men reported feeling some guilt during the affair, yet it didn't stop them. Seventeen percent experienced guilt only at the onset of the affair, 31 percent experienced guilt throughout the affair, and 18 percent said the guilt escalated as the affair continued. The rest of the men, 34 percent, did not experience any guilt at any point in the affair. Hard to imagine. Even if cheating men feel guilty, they often have a way of seeing an affair as some sort of repercussion of a bad marriage. Man after man told me things like, "Hey, it's going to happen if things aren't right at home. It doesn't make it right but that's how it happens." Most of them felt guilty, but the idea that cheating was an allowable consequence to a "failed" marriage won out. Clearly, if the husband felt his wife was cheating, all bets were off and guilt didn't even enter the picture.

Trying to create guilt won't help to protect your marriage. Reminding your husband from time to time how much you'll hurt if he ever cheats is far from a proven anticheating method. Talking about how bad it is in conversation with friends as a way to let your husband know how you feel about it won't work. He knows it's bad and chances are he'll feel guilty if he chooses to have an affair. It's more important to remember that your husband is likely not as strong as you want to think. He doesn't take criticism well and will likely back away when he feels disapproved of. Put him in a situation where he feels he can't win and watch how he steps back and begins to see his relationship with another woman as an evolving repercussion of a no-win situation. Be aware to try and give him the opportunity to do the right thing for you and be appreciative of his effort even though he doesn't necessarily hit the mark. Don't give him the excuses he'll use to dispel his guilt, citing your lack of warmth and appreciation.

The Ones Who Will Cheat No Matter What

One of the most disturbing parts of my research was that 12 percent of the cheating men said it had nothing to do with any dissatisfaction in their marriage. On the one hand, it's refreshing to know that 88 percent of men who cheated felt that had the marriage been different in some way (and this is not to say that they had no hand in that), they would not have cheated. This gives much hope for most wives that making the effort toward creating a successful marriage using the techniques we're discussing will result in a wonderful, protected marriage. But for the wives married to the other 12 percent, it seems like they might be spinning their wheels. This isn't completely true, however. When I interviewed these men, they didn't feel that any dissatisfaction in their marriage served as a catalyst to their cheating. But some of them were clear in feeling that if the marriage were different in some way, they might have stayed be faithful. They did believe (and for some it was borne out in their minds through faithfulness in later marriages) that had the marriage been one where they felt more connected, things would've have been different, even if that only meant they would've agreed to get professional help if their wives had demanded it.

For a wife who is married to this type of man, finding out about the affair and separating as soon as possible might be the smartest solution. These men are cheating because they are cheaters from the very start (regardless of the deeper psychological or cultural reasons that may have developed this behavior in them). Short of extreme remorse, a commitment to intensive psychotherapy, and a willingness to allow for ongoing detection (regular lie-detector tests . . .), the pain of staying with that man would seem to outweigh the odds of a complete change to fidelity.

QUICK ACTION PROGRAM

Step Four: Practice Emotional Giving

We've learned that the number one issue surrounding the cheating factor is emotional dissatisfaction, specifically lack of appreciation. This is the first place where you want to take action.

Consider appreciation:

1. How do you think you do in this area? Rate yourself (on a scale of 1 to 10).

2. How would your husband rate you on an appreciation scale? Rate yourself (on a scale of 1 to 10).

3. List examples of things you did in the past two weeks to show your appreciation—*gestures your husband would recognize as appreciation.* (For example, he wouldn't say that your caring for the kids is considered an appreciative gesture toward him.)

4. Create an appreciation list about your husband (after you've recognized that he is to be appreciated for things he is responsible for doing anyway). What about him do you appreciate?

5. List the top five ways you think your husband would say he'd like for you to show your appreciation. Take quick action by doing these five things for him.

Now that you've put your thoughts together on the subject, consider taking the following emotional giving action steps.

Starting today, once a day, I will verbalize an appreciative comment:

1. A simple thank-you for any gesture my husband makes.

2. An expression of thanks for his hard work in general.

3. A thank-you for a recently attained work-related goal.

4. Appreciation for accomplishing a personal goal for me or the kids (thanks for getting my car fixed, helping your child with his project, calling the phone company to straighten out my mom's service, etc.).

Starting today, once a day, I will offer a warm and kind gesture to show my appreciation without verbal comment. He will just feel appreciated and loved from these gestures without them being attached to any specific thing he's done. Examples:

1. A tender kiss.

2. A warm hug.

3. A small gift (magazine, food item) that he particularly likes.

Starting this week, twice a week, I will offer a more involved gesture. For only one of these two gestures, I will tell him I'm doing this to appreciate him for something specific he's done (it can be general or specific as long as it is spoken either immediately before or after the gesture). "I thought you'd like this because: you've been working so hard lately/have been so nice to me/really helped me so much with my work situation yesterday/have really picked up the slack since I've been working late recently/have been thoughtful while I was sick."

Examples of the two thoughtful gestures I'll begin to offer this week and continue in the coming weeks:

1. Preparing a special meal, something he loves to eat.

2. Touching him more lovingly.

3. Arranging an evening out with him.

4. Arranging a special evening with him in mind (tickets to a sporting event with me or with a friend of his or your child).

What if he hasn't been so nice, warm, or hard working? Avoid trying to tell him what he *didn't* do (he likely won't be receptive anyway) and focus on what he *did*. Stick to your Quick Action Program and really appreciate even the small things he does that are positive. Try it for one week. If you were sick and he could have done a lot better, still appreciate him for the small things he did do. Chances are you'll soon have a husband who wants to please you more than ever.

5

The Power of Sex

As we've seen, sex is not the main motivator of cheating men. With a miniscule 8 percent of men telling us that sexual dissatisfaction was the primary factor that figured into their cheating, it makes little sense to focus only on great sex as a means to creating a protected marriage. Without a huge push and consistent focus on the emotional side of your husband, sex won't be nearly enough. It makes sense, of course, as we all figure that sex for the sake of sex alone really isn't all it's cracked up to be. Yes, we know sexual skill can make a big difference in the bedroom. But in marriage, it's the emotional part of things that makes us want to please each other, work at sex, show our appreciation by venturing into areas we'd otherwise leave behind. Without the emotional component, a couple is left with a lack of sexual satisfaction even if both partners might be "great at sex."

So changing your sexual lifestyle by itself isn't the right move. However, let's not confuse ourselves and think that the cheating men were saying sex had little to do with their cheating. Yes, it is absolutely clear that 48 percent of the men said it was emotional dissatisfaction in the marriage that was the primary factor leading them to cheating. Another way of looking at it might be that 48 percent of the men were telling us that if they felt more emotionally connected to their wives, they would not have cheated. That is why the first focus of this book and your personal effort to build a protected and solid marriage should be to put energy into understanding yourself and finding new and better ways to build the emotional side of your marriage.

But keep in mind that 32 percent of the men in my research responded that *both* emotional dissatisfaction and an unsatisfying sexual relationship figured about the same in their decision to cheat. These men tell us that it isn't all about sex but it isn't not about sex either. If we were to take this 32 percent and add to it the 8 percent of men who did say it was about sexual dissatisfaction, we would be left with 40 percent who told us sex weighed heavily into their cheating even if it was not the primary contributor.

But the big remaining question was what it was about sex that the men found particularly dissatisfying.

James's Story: He Wanted More Sex

James was one of the few cheaters who cited sexual dissatisfaction as the primary issue in his marriage. "All of my friends and I used to sit around joking about how marriage killed our sex lives and I told my wife that I wanted more sex. But I also told her I didn't want her to just give in and do it because I said so. She had gained some weight after our third child was born and was very self-conscious, which made her want sex even less. But she seemed to really hear me because she started working out and dieting really seriously, and within six months or so she really got her body back, really looked good. But it didn't matter.

"Sex was pretty good when we had it, but between the kids and her work she was always exhausted and just wasn't into sex at all. We still argued about it and she still said it was my fault, and maybe it was.

"When my wife found out about the affair she felt horrible. She immediately felt it was because she wasn't sexy enough, and I swore to her that the other woman was not prettier. As a matter of fact, she didn't have as nice a body as my wife had. But she was available. I really wasn't expecting sex to be so incredible with my wife every time, but I needed to have sex regularly and it had to be a little exciting. If that had happened, I don't think I would've cheated. I know how much she tried but it just wasn't happening. I just couldn't see myself spending the rest of my life having sex once in a while."

Imagine James's wife. As she's working harder to "change" her sexual image, her husband is still getting closer to having an affair. This woman's focus likely could have been spent in a different area of her sex life, and it would have given her better odds of finding happiness with him in bed.

In my questionnaire, I asked the following. "These were the specific sexual issues that factored into my infidelity." The possible responses were:

- Sex with my wife was unsatisfying
- My wife had significantly neglected her appearance
- Sex with my wife was generally too infrequent
- Other

I'd be curious to know what you wrote to answer the question on page 12, because I think this is one area women can get fooled about. Whenever you read women's magazines, the focus is on "hot sex" and what you had better do to make your man happy. The media messages are clear: if you're not in model shape with the best that plastic surgery has to offer and a PhD in Prostitution Ed., it's no wonder your man will stray. It's as if you can't blame the poor guy for having to put up with the missionary position or stretch marks. Men have messages enveloping them that seem to scream, "Why doesn't your wife look like this?" and "Why doesn't your wife call you in the middle of the day and suggest risqué adventures? Have men taken the bait and raised the bar of sex to the degree that you'd better spend two hours a day working out and starving yourself and spend another two or three hours a day just thinking about how to please your husband sexually? Kids? Let 'em get their own meals. Your income? Who needs it? At least your food bill will decrease because you'll be subsisting on ten daily almonds.

With a sigh of relief, I'm proud to report that men have not yet been manipulated to demand the things that the media would like you to believe. Here are the results of this part of the questionnaire.

"Other" got 11 percent, the lowest percentage. "My wife had significantly neglected her appearance" came in at only 15 percent. "Sex with my wife was unsatisfying" came in at 26 percent. The number one answer was, "Sex with my wife was generally too infrequent," at 48 percent.

That is a huge number. Before you go to the gym, diet, and get the *Kama Sutra*, make it easy on yourself. "Often" is the winner, at least when you're discussing keeping a marriage strong.

I imagine you put a strong number next to the frequency option in your guess, but you likely placed larger numbers next to the other two options than the research showed. What a relief to know that once again you don't have to believe the advertisers who want you to buy stuff.

I Don't Get the Sex Thing

Carol's Story: Sexual Resentment

Carol was one of many women over the years who've shared with me her perplexity at the sex thing. She felt that all she needed to do was give her husband sex and he'd be nice. If not, he'd be distant and difficult. She felt cheapened and was downright angry about it by the time she spoke with me. She felt she offered little to her husband. It was all about being a receptacle, or as she graphically put it, his "sperm toilet." She felt that any woman could be that. It seemed to her the only thing her husband ever thought about. After sex, he could be there for her in so many ways, but until she'd give in, he could think or talk to her of nothing else. In fact, he had cheated on her when they were engaged. She had entered the marriage with an anxious feeling that she'd better put out to protect her marriage, and she resented every minute of it. She was like so many women who don't get the sex thing and resent that their spouse's mood is dependent on their willingness to be a sex partner.

For over twenty years I've heard wives lament the very same issues about sex. "Why is it if I give him sex he's all nice to me? If I don't give him sex, he's obnoxious. That's not right. I hate that."

They make a good point. If a partner doesn't want to engage in an activity requested by the other partner, all hell shouldn't break loose. But we must revisit the fact that every relationship is a give-and-take. We each have to bring things to the table that please our spouse. If he didn't do something you loved enough, you might be distant or upset too.

Women love to be loved. You'd like your husband to smile widely at you, look into your eyes, hug you, and tell you that you're the best thing that ever happened to him. If he did that, I hope you'd feel more kindly toward him, more willing to please him, and motivated to give more to him. Maybe your mood would be much better. So when your husband complains that when you came home you were in a sour mood, what's wrong with you saying to him, "You know what kind of hellish day I had? Maybe if you would've greeted me with a kiss and a little appreciation or offer to help I would've been different." And if he responds with, "So it's all just about a kiss and giving you a half hour of help? If I don't spend the time or at least offer, you're in a bad mood and not nice to me?" then he's not understanding or properly caring, is he? That's because you understand that he is responsible for helping you get over the rough edges of life and adding immeasurably to the good moments as well. That is why you married him.

Guess what? This is what he wants to tell you about sex. He wants you to understand that's it's a primary way for him to feel loved and have pleasure, and yes, when you offer it it'll likely place him in a better, sweeter mood—the same way his offering you a caring gesture will likely place you in a better, sweeter mood.

Harold was one faithful man who explained how much sex could mean to a man on a personal level. "I probably have a very different story from most men. I was this pimply, nerdy teenager, and even in college I was so shy I felt like no girl would want me. By the time I met my wife I only had some self-esteem because I had done really well for myself and had a little money. But I was still painfully shy. I really think it was the sex that helped me change. When my wife wanted me in that way as often as she did, it really made me feel successful in a way I had never felt before. It was like she proved to me that she really liked me and found me attractive. For our first few years together I probably didn't talk too much unless it was around sex. It was at the point of knowing she still was attracted to me that I felt comfortable enough telling her about my day and feeling that she was listening and not going to judge me. I was very worried about any criticism and when she wanted to make love to me, it let me know she approved of me. From that I was able to trust her."

Why Sex?

"Hold on," you say. "Sex is way different from what I ask of him."

Indeed, you may see a clear distinction between the simple, loving gestures you want and the sex that your husband wants. Sex is an extremely intimate gesture, not something a woman just whips up, and you may feel that the loving comment and thoughtful gesture you desire from your husband is not nearly as intimate. Actually, for many men, being emotionally present and offering these loving gestures is being extraordinarily intimate and requires major energy and focus, even though it's not to be equated with your effort to make love to him.

This doesn't mean you shouldn't expect meaningful warmth from your husband. It just means his effort to offer you intimacy can require a great deal of focus and energy. Your husband being constantly aroused and desiring sex with you is not insulting or demeaning. That sexual intimacy might help him express more love or kindness to you does not make him a pig.

In fact, your husband is not much different from you. Even though you may want different actions, both of you want the same thing: loving, pleasing gestures from your lover.

There is clearly a difference between the sexes in the way sexuality works. I think it is a myth that men are more into sex. Rather, I think men are more into sex for sex's sake than women, who can love sex but need emotional stimulation and love to be inherent in the experience. Men can be easily sexually stimulated by pure physical sexual thoughts or sights, whereas women are more likely to be stimulated by some emotional connection. This is why it is far more likely that a man will have an erection if physically stimulated even without emotional connection whereas a woman can be physically touched and yet remain numb if there is a lack of it. This doesn't mean that a man's pleasure and desires are not significantly increased with the attachment of an emotional connection. They are.

Women sometimes feel cheap because they think that his desire for sex has little or nothing to do with them. It's a physical thing, like eating. Many wives feel it's not so much about them as it is about his raw needs. This can definitely take the joy out of sex for any woman.

My research clearly showed that men wanted an emotional relationship more than anything else, so we've learned that women don't have a monopoly on desire for an emotional connection. Yes, men think sexual thoughts far more often than women and could likely have unemotional sex more easily than women, but they recognize that great sex with someone who isn't into them emotionally, who doesn't "get them," is a short-lived relationship. They may talk a big sex game, but what they really want is a woman who loves and desires them. That's why any man would hate to think that his wife is just having sex for him and she couldn't care less. If she doesn't like it or doesn't really want to have it but does her duty, this doesn't work for men. He wants to make love regularly as much as you do. The fact that it may start with a raw, physical hunger doesn't mean he wants to fill himself with a raw, physical, emotionally distant solution.

This explains why it's not such an easy option for him to "take care of himself," as many women have expressed to me. He could and possibly does masturbate at times. And if it was all about release and nothing more, nothing emotional about it, then he'd be a happy camper by himself. But the men we interviewed wanted much more than just a release. They want to feel desired, attractive, connected to someone who is happy to receive and give pleasure in an act reserved only for the two of you.

Making Sex Work for Both of You

Often, because there is a greater raw, physical need for men, sex sometimes becomes more about intercourse than for a woman. Women usually report looking for more hugs, cuddling, kissing, and foreplay than their husbands do. Here is where you can make a great difference in your sex life. Too often women allow their husbands to take the lead in the bedroom and are left unsatisfied. Soon, sex is largely about him, and it can quickly become a chore for any wife. Left to his own devices, he may fall far short of pleasing you, because he's not a woman, and I don't care how many sex partners you think or he says he's had before you, it doesn't make him an expert. So if you've left your sexual fulfillment in your husband's hands and you feel it could be much better, it's time for you to make it so.

Here is the greatest benefit of your husband's raw, physical need for sex; he's pretty happy with anything you bring to it. He's into sex enough that if you want to take the lead, slow it down, help him please you, he's likely to be genuinely thrilled. If you want more foreplay, more hugs and kisses before going further, his sexual energy will carry him quite far in pleasing you. You can create a relationship that works for both of you, but it'll take some effort on your part. I don't mean to say that you have to feel that you're in charge every time you fool around. Of course you like to be made love to without having to be directing every moment. But sexual partners are responsible for training each other just like in every other part of the relationship, and at times they must continue to help their partner hone his or her skills.

If you are hesitant to take any sort of control over your sex life or focus on your own pleasure during sex, consider why you feel this way. Perhaps this results from the societal messages women are given that it's both unladylike and embarrassing for a woman to really love and enjoy sex. This could be why 43 percent of all women suffer from some sexual dysfunction.

Most likely, your husband will be very willing and happy to please you. Most men are turned on by the thought of being able to please their wives and enjoy doing whatever it takes to make this happen.

Imagine if your sexual experience was pretty good for you most every time. Now that you've learned it's really not about the sex but the emotional connection even from your husband's point of view, can you see yourself increasing the frequency of sex with your husband? Can you now see it as simply showing your husband your happiness and showing him love through making love with him? That's all it really is. And believe it or not, once you increase the frequency through this giving and personal enjoyment, he will not complain about it and have that "never enough" attitude. Yes, there are men who have enough sex, who feel fulfilled sexually even though they may be happy to have more. When they feel their wives are really hearing them on the sex issue and wanting to give to them through this act, they become content.

Making Sex Work for *You*

Your pleasure during intimacy is crucial to your comfort and willing-ness to increase sexual frequency with your husband. At this point, I'd like to have the freedom to speak rather graphically. It may be information you already know. But through my twenty years of mari-tal counseling this simple, necessary piece of information has been the most effective way of quickly helping married couples' sex lives.

The vast majority (anywhere from 50 to 75 percent according to WebMD.com and DrPhil.com) of women do not reach orgasm through vaginal stimulation, which means chances are that simple intercourse will not cause you to achieve orgasm. This doesn't mean that there isn't pleasure in it for you from both a biological and emotional perspective. But it likely rates low on the enjoyment scale. There is one part of your body, though, that has the most nerve endings per area of anywhere on the male or female body: the clitoris, the small knob of skin that forms at the top of the vaginal opening. I've been surprised to discover how many men and women are unaware of how important this part of the body is to the female orgasm. I have had occasion to share this information with male doctors who still were unfamiliar with this territory. The bottom line is that the vast majority of women need clitoral stimulation in order to reach orgasm.

The problem is that simple intercourse is rarely going to stimulate the clitoris, leaving too many wives without the intense pleasure that would create a more fulfilling lovemaking experience. Books will have you try all kinds of different positions in order to make valiant attempts at getting your husband's penis to somehow touch this part of your body, but frankly, it ain't easy. The simplest and smartest way of increasing your pleasure is by you or your husband stimulating your clitoris before and during intercourse. This would mean that you'd be in a sexual position that allows the space for your or your husband's hand to be touching your clitoris. This has many advantages, as it intensifies your pleasure and allows for more joint control over your pleasure. You can speed it up or slow it down depending on the amount of stimulation you like.

If you are uncomfortable with this, start considering why (we'll discuss it in the next chapter with the Inner Voice Recognition Formula). Some women have shared with me that they feel embarrassed and uncomfortable with creating such pleasure for themselves, as if it's cheating, and that they should be able to just have an orgasm through intercourse. You'll want to consider the Inner Voice Recognition Formula to try to see the emotional issues wrapped up in any resistance you may have to this idea. But this is the only physical technique I'll outline, because it is the one worth putting all your effort into when it comes to learning how to make lovemaking best for you.

If you are in any way unfamiliar with your own clitoris, it would be wise, normal, and very common for you to learn about it by yourself in order to know how it feels and then be able to help yourself orgasm during lovemaking. Eighty-nine percent of women report that they have masturbated, so it is clearly normal. Additionally, many women find that a vibrator is helpful and easier for them to use to achieve orgasm through clitoral stimulation. The good news is that you no longer need to face the uncomfortable journey into a sex shop in order to purchase a vibrator. There was an episode on *Sex and the City* where the women joked about the vibrators available at stores like Brookstone and Sharper Image, penlike massagers that can be used for clitoral stimulation. If you find using a vibrator easier and more comfortable, use it during intercourse as well. Your husband will probably be delighted.

If you'd like or prefer your husband to stimulate your clitoris during sex, you'll need to direct him, as there's no way you could expect him to know how to stimulate you in a way that feels best for you. It is common for a wife to do this during intercourse—not with graphs and maps but either through simple voice tones of "there," "softer," or "a little harder," or by simply moving his finger into a spot that is best for you. And you might need to continue giving some direction because at different moments you may want different pressure. Although some women don't like the idea of having to direct traffic during lovemaking, it's necessary to a point if you'd like your husband to stimulate your clitoris instead of you doing it yourself. When the clitoris is stimulated, intercourse causes a heightened intensity to your orgasm. You and your husband can always rest assured that intercourse is still a crucial part of your orgasm as the vaginal walls will also register pleasure and the emotional connectedness of intercourse will heighten your pleasure.

Have Sex That Works for You

Most women do not reach orgasm through vaginal stimulation.

1. Before and during intercourse, use clitoral stimulation.

2. Get your needs met from your husband (loving touch, loving verbalization, focusing on getting you close to orgasm) before he orgasms.

Lessen the Gender Discrepancies

To make lovemaking work best for you as well as your husband, you will need to level the playing field. Remember, men tend to orgasm much faster than women. The average woman takes anywhere from twelve to twenty minutes to orgasm, while the average man takes anywhere from one minute to just over seven minutes with steady vaginal thrusting. Most men will take longer to orgasm if they're having sex more frequently, but it's unlikely they'll catch up to their wives.

This discrepancy has wreaked havoc on the sex lives of couples. Too often men are rushing to the intercourse part, which means the clock is ticking and if you are not close to an orgasm there is an excellent chance he will climax before you. Soon after his orgasm, his penis will likely become flaccid and you may feel unfulfilled. Either of you could continue to stimulate your clitoris, but after one of you has an orgasm the level of willingness to please the other quickly diminishes.

While a man is sexually excited, though, he's usually willing to be extremely attentive to his wife's sexual desires. Don't pass up this opportunity to make sex work better for you. Your best bet is to make sure you get the most out of your foreplay while your husband is in the mood. I'm not only talking about him pleasing you sexually. I mean, if you want more of the emotional side of sex, like more kissing, more 'I love you's, more hugging . . . the time to get it and have it work for you is before he has had or is well on his way to an orgasm. Plus if you stick to your guns and keep him focused on pleasing you with loving words and touches, he will soon learn that this is part of your collective lovemaking technique and it'll create a sexual frequency that will be ultimately pleasing for both of you. This doesn't mean that every time you make love there'll be fireworks. But it means that most of the time both of you will be generally satisfied and have orgasms. Keep in mind that my research found that frequency was much more important than how fantastic the actual sex rated.

Get Yourself Ready While He Takes a Break

Throughout my years of counseling couples, I've learned another common obstacle to a satisfying sexual relationship for women. A wife will stimulate her husband whether manually or orally and then immediately after, they'll have intercourse. Because the man has already been somewhat stimulated his likelihood of having an orgasm rather quickly during intercourse is increased. Too often, even with clitoral stimulation, the wife can't get herself quite there and becomes frustrated when her husband climaxes and she's not nearly as close to an orgasm as she wanted to be.

A simple solution is to focus on sexual foreplay for your husband, then have him take a break and focus on you sexually for a while before intercourse. This way, intercourse will begin with you already on your way to having an orgasm and he'll be starting after a break, giving him more time before having an orgasm. Again, you'll likely need to have your clitoris stimulated during intercourse in order for you to climax. Also, it's your job to let your husband know that you need a bit more time: ask him to slow his thrusting depending on how much time you need and let him know to thrust faster or in a way that helps you reach an orgasm. This way, he'll be able to somewhat extend the time before he orgasms.

He's not the mind reader you'd like him to be, and as long as the end result is that he feels he's pleased you, he'll be more than happy to hear a word of direction and encouragement along the way.

Lock Your Bedroom Door

You have a statistically greater possibility of having sex more often if you touch each other more. It makes sense that the more we physically touch each other, the more comfortable we become with physical intimacy. Yet there is an immense amount of time that you could be physically connecting to your husband that you're losing due to your identity as a guilt-ridden parent.

Because you have been made to feel by society that no matter how much love and attention you give your children it will fall short of what they ideally need, you (like everyone) feel a certain bit of guilt when you participate in some life activity that excludes the kids. I am not suggesting that any of us should be gallivanting around feeding our selfish pursuits while our children go hungry for our attention. I have strong, close friendships with each of my five kids. Yet I have struggled with that sense of guilt that all of us are subject to when we want to consistently exclude our children from certain parts of our marriage. Sure, we're okay with the principle of excluding them and taking a parents-only vacation every once in a blue moon. But when it comes to regular uninterrupted time alone as parents to do adult things, we have to wonder if we are neglecting our children in some way.

Over the last twenty years, I've become more insistent about creating a marital atmosphere that is isolated from everything else: children and business. We spend approximately seven and a half hours sleeping each night. Multiply that by 365 days in a year and you have about 2,737 hours. Add to it the hours before bedtime when you may frequently need to complete tasks, wind down, or get ready for bed, and you're easily over 3,000 hours per year. I know many of you don't have a spare minute, but in truth, there are stages of life where we do have some downtime if we allow ourselves—and don't forget the old idea that if you needed to find some extra time for a crucial pursuit that your child needed, the time would magically appear.

Your husband knows you're busy. But he also knows that if you had to find time to cuddle your child more, read with him, and work on his social skills through guided activities, in addition to the work you do at the office or caring for your home, you'd find it. And therefore he can't help but wonder how not to take it as a message of "You're not important enough, I don't appreciate you that much" when you can't find the time to be intimate with him. Perhaps he doesn't understand when you are bone tired due to pregnancy, PMS, exhausting nights with a sick child, and an endless list of life's stresses. But he does know that all of us must make time for what is important to us. If we can't, we need to get help, and the first step would be discussing with him that you want to be more intimate but need help in finding the answers for how to create that relaxed time. That shows your desire to be with him and enjoy him, as well as your commitment to finding solutions to make it happen.

How do you create this block of time to connect with your husband in order to enjoy each other and create more opportunity for greater sexual frequency? Consider how much time your children have your attention. Then consider how much it means to your children to have their parents in love and not divorced. These are two serious ways to counter the guilt you may begin to feel if you exclude your children from adult time on a regular basis. Take into account the message you'll be sending your children when you exclude them from your bedroom at night, even if only for you and your husband to talk uninterruptedly—the real message would be that adult lovers need interactive time that is just for them. That would be a wonderful model for them as they grow and look to succeed in their own marriages. All of this leads to the idea of finding regular nightly time to connect emotionally and physically.

"I joked that our bedroom should have a revolving door," Mitch told me when lamenting his infrequent sex life. Mitch tried to tell his wife he needed some space with her, but "she'd explain that we had to make the kids feel secure, and I agreed. I love my kids like crazy and want them to feel very comfortable around us. I wasn't so close to my parents and I surely didn't mind doing things differently."

But it didn't make Mitch or his wife very happy. Except for a rare three-day cruise alone, they never felt like they had any space for just the two of them. Who could possibly be passionately in love and have a warm, meaningful marriage without any space to make it happen?

What would happen to your children if you locked your bedroom door at night? When they are teenagers and are alone in their room would they not be entitled to close their doors? They'd be entitled to do so if you trusted they weren't doing anything that conflicted with the rules of your home. They're not shutting you out so much as properly seeking privacy for certain parts of their lives. Your children will only feel shut out of your life if you are not emotionally there for them. Closing your door or leaving it wide open will not speak to that. You can have your door taken off its hinges and have an incredibly distant relationship with your children.

Closing your door at night with a simple rule that your children can knock in the middle of the night if there is a problem (fear, illness) teaches them to respect your privacy and sleep. It also teaches them to be able to take care of small issues in the night by themselves. Once they knock you can choose to let them in to sleep with you or return them to their bed.

Over my years of helping couples, I've learned from many that they don't lock their bedroom doors when they're making love. There are some who even have sex with their doors open. I've heard all kinds of similar reasons. "We only do it after the kids are asleep." "We can hear them coming up the steps, down the hall." But without knowing it these couples are having sex with the conscious concern that their children might come in or be on their way at any moment. This means someone is listening, serving as a lookout, whether you're actively focused on it or not. This has got to take away from your focus on making love whether you realize it or not. Sex becomes reduced to something quite inhibited, stifled, and silent.

If you locked your bedroom door at night, the two of you could sleep in a much more relaxed manner (such as naked) and create a space for intimacy for 2,737 hours a year plus the time before sleep and waking up. This doesn't mean you'd be having regular sex in the middle of the night—that's unusual for most couples—but it sets the stage for a certain area of privacy that reminds you both that you belong to each other and share an intimacy that is private to both of you. It means you can cuddle at moments in the night and feel each other's skin, a sense of warm contact instead of touching a child or the soft cotton of your lover's sleeping wardrobe. You don't have to worry about your children catching you in compromising positions or states of undress. You buy yourself a lifetime of intimacy that doesn't need to lead anywhere tonight or tomorrow but does give both of you that feeling of being lovers that so easily disappears in our busy world. Plus, it allows you to have sex in the morning if you both wake early, without the concern that the kids will surprise you.

If your younger children currently sleep in your bed, compromise with them by either giving them positive rewards for staying in their own beds or offering them one night on a weekend where they can sleep and "camp out" in your room (regularly at first) when everyone can enjoy cuddling with each other for the night. I'm all for family bed cuddling, but this can be achieved while reading or watching television together on given nights. It doesn't have to translate to sharing your bed.

Feel Comfortable in Your Bedroom

When making love while your kids are in the house, even if the kids are asleep, turn on some music or the TV so that you can feel more comfortable with noise surrounding your lovemaking and worry less that the kids will hear. This can create a much more enjoyable sexual experience for you, which in turn will motivate you to have more sex with your husband. Find time to initiate sex when the kids are not in the house, perhaps after they've left for school, if your husband is still around.

The bottom line: whatever you can do to ensure lovemaking is nicer for yourself, work on it and your husband will most likely be thrilled to help. Create a bedroom atmosphere that is warm and beautiful. Get wonderful sheets, a great mattress, pleasant bed-clothes, and artwork to make this spot in your life a pleasant one that you and your husband largely share only with each other.

Make Time for Love

Create privacy by:

1. Locking your bedroom door at night.

2. Turning up the music during lovemaking.

3. Focusing on intimacy outside the bedroom by giving your husband more loving hugs and kisses, back rubs, foot massages etc. He'll respond by being more loving to you throughout your day.

Keep Your Bathroom Behavior Private

Here's another consideration while you are wondering how you can have more frequent sex: many couples live a lifestyle that allows for regular sighting of their spouse using the bathroom facilities. Don't! All of us understand the reality of life and time management, two people sharing a bathroom, rushed and hurried. But this doesn't mean that over the long haul observing our spouse in less than appealing situations won't take its toll. Keep in mind that reality will dictate that we will already have to see our spouse in compromising positions. There will be illness and procedures and plenty of physical ailments that will more than fill our cups with the real world. But those tend to be inconsistent and chalked up to necessity. When you regularly view your husband on the toilet, it can add up to a vision that directly or indirectly diminishes your sexual attraction. I'm all for realness between couples and am not suggesting that people should hide ailments or weaknesses. But you are entitled to clean up his act and request that there be private bathroom time with a little respectful time-management cooperation, that he be prepared for sex with a cleanliness quotient that works for you, and that he stop any adolescent humor that is a turn-off for you. Many women explain all this away with a "boys will be boys" attitude. But we've learned that statistically your husband is looking much more for appreciation and sex and would be thrilled to forgo any boyish behavior if he felt it served a genuine effort on your part to be more connected to him. This is where you can become more in control of your marital destiny without being emasculating. Take measures into your own hands and help change the areas that may be distracting you from a pleasing lovemaking lifestyle.

The Role of Childhood Abuse

It's a sad fact that there is way too much sexual molestation in our world—statistics claim that one out of three children is inappropriately touched. As far as we believe we've come to protect our children, we are light-years away from where we need to be. There is so much cover-up in too many situations that allow our youngsters to suffer a pain that will last a lifetime. Let's not forget that molestation goes beyond the awful, vicious types of inappropriateness. It extends to less vicious abuse like inappropriate touching over clothing . . . the kinds of things that get explained away too often by parents who convince their kids that they "were mistaken, they just accidentally bumped into you." The world continues to neglect the unimaginable sadness and pain of young people who have to grow into adults carrying complex feelings of sexual dirtiness and unbearable guilt.

Molestation causes at the very least sexual hang-ups, whether promiscuity or extreme avoidance of sex—in any case, a severe discomfort with sexuality. Sometimes you can remember what happened, and other times you've blocked the painful memories out and can't understand why you don't like sex. You might find other rational reasons for avoiding sexual pleasure, like "There's no time," "He doesn't do what I want," "I'm too shy to let him down there," "It's all so messy, who knows?" But you may really be avoiding a painful place in your life that no one and for now even you can't understand. If you find yourself wondering and struggling with this possibility, do yourself a favor and be self-deserving enough to talk to someone in your area who's an expert in this field. Don't allow the bad people from your past to continue to molest you and rob you of good life moments that you deserve and need to take back for yourself. Be kind to yourself.

Victims of molestation often have to feel as if they're in control when returning to healthy adult sexuality. In order to turn off the ugliness of the past, you'll want to explain to your husband that for a while, you'll need to take control, determine positions, say when and where, and, most of all, have him okay with stopping at any point if you're feeling uncomfortable emotionally. He'll need to understand why, of course, and he'll likely be comfortable with allowing you to be in charge while you work to allow yourself to be whole again.

Use Birth Control That Puts Your Mind at Ease

Many women have shared with me that their concern about becoming pregnant weighs on their minds. If you don't want to get pregnant now, it's important to be thinking about birth control when you're going to have sex. You may not think it's on your mind, but unless you are confident in your birth control methods your mind will subtly direct you away from good, frequent sex. Be sure that if you are unsure of the birth control methods you're using, sex is a latent enemy. Figure this one out, whether through thorough education and conversations with your doctor or clear talk with your husband about what you need from him if he's assigned as the purveyor of birth control. Explain that you don't want any mistakes, and again, help him understand that if he takes this as seriously as you do, you can be more relaxed about it all—and that will translate to more lovemaking and fun for both of you.

Take Sexuality Seriously

When you take sex seriously and understand that it is about an intimacy that is crucial and a feeling of appreciation for your husband, you can begin to prioritize it. Again, I'm not asking you to do a hundred different things. Developing a more frequent sexual lifestyle is a necessary ingredient to happy marriages. Unfortunately, if we wait for sex to find us spontaneously, we'll be waiting a long time. As much as we'd like to have this naturally passionate lifestyle, you'll need to forgo those unrealistic Hollywood visions and learn to carve out these moments from the real world you live in. Plan an evening when you can be alone in your room. Tell your husband that you'd like him to help you get the kids to bed at a decent hour so the two of you can spend time alone. It doesn't have to always mean sex, but if it's working well for both of you, it's likely you'll get there and want to make an effort to get there more and more.

PART TWO

How to Improve Your Marriage

6

Insightful Change: The Inner Voice Recognition Formula

We're past reporting what contributes to men cheating. Now you will get clear answers about what you can do about it. But knowing how to solve a problem doesn't mean you will. Just because research tells you to be appreciative and thoughtful toward your husband doesn't mean you're going to wrap your arms around him, rent a hotel room for the night, or cook him his favorite meal when he walks through the door tonight.

The Many Voices We House Within

Our voices change and we commonly don't hear it. A friend clues us in with a "What's wrong, it sounds like you're sick." If we're happy or sad, awake or tired, it'll directly affect our communication pattern and we don't even realize it. If that's what's happening on the outside where you can physically hear yourself, imagine what's going on on the inside. Indeed, you have many voices within clamoring to speak, and depending on myriad issues, a specific voice will get first billing and lead you on your way. The problem is, we call this our reaction as though it just is and there's not much we can do about it. That's where we are wrong. We *can* begin to learn which voices we use when different situations come our way.

For years, I've been helping people to try to understand the root of their struggles—the *why* behind their often illogical actions—in order to assist them in real, qualitative change. Too often, people have been made to believe that no one can change, a wonderfully rationalizing thought that seems to forgive our unwillingness to challenge ourselves. You *can* change. Any part of yourself that you don't like or that is not working for you is in your power to change. To believe differently is to question the very basis of being human. We are different from the rest of the animal world because of our ability to think and feel on a level that allows us to change and adapt.

The process of really making significant changes comes with a great deal of time and insight. For years I've worked at helping couples understand themselves and better their marriages. But maintaining that ability to see personal issues and sustain changes outside of my office or seminar, when I wasn't present to clarify their unique issues, proved too often to be a real challenge. And since I chose not to live with any of the people I had helped and become their twenty-four-hour-a-day marital therapist, I searched for a way to help them take the therapy with them into their own worlds.

Marriage counseling, more than any other form of counseling, is different because speed is everything. There isn't a great deal of time to make changes as a marriage is faltering. I want to avoid the psychobabble and help people get right to the heart of every marital issue and be able to deal with it and make quick positive changes. Until you can understand why you truly feel a certain way and act on it, you have little chance of following through with any behavioral change. It's not enough to just assume you'll follow a direction because it is logical or stated in a book.

I've boiled this insight process down to a relatively simple formula that allows you to understand your internal struggle and make changes much quicker than you'd imagine. I'm not saying that this formula is all my own. But understanding in my own way, I've been able to express a lot of complicated truths that you can then put together into a palatable package that can allow you to sift through insights and make changes immediately.

Your Brain Can Hamper You

Your brain is amazing. You have about 70,000 thoughts per day. Your central nervous system, though, tosses out 99 percent of what your senses register so as not to bother your brain with unimportant matters. You shouldn't expect to understand more than 70 percent of what you hear. The brain automatically fills in the gaps. It is those gaps you want to start getting better acquainted with, because they are based on many events that have happened in your life and your brain is not clueing you in to them.

One great example of how our brains work is reading. You don't sound out every word. You notice the first letter or two and, based on the context of the content, your brain makes a leap and guesses the word. And your brain does a pretty good job most of the time.

This is what your mind is doing when it is *emotionally reading* a situation as well. It recognizes the context of the situation based on your personal history and present surroundings and then makes leaps and guesses. Because your reaction feels as natural as reading words on a page, you rarely slow it down to seriously consider whether you've gotten the context and content right.

But this is what I will ask you to do. In order to better your marriage, you need to recognize that you've been emotionally reading situations and making leaps and guesses without properly understanding the full context and content. Your brain has been on autopilot, helping you process while tossing out as much as it can. When you take control, slow down, and begin to recognize more and more what is causing your reactions, that's when you can make the best changes and significantly improve your emotional reading. You won't have to guess any longer.

Which Voice Are You Activating?

Imagine for a moment that there are three voices in your head whenever you confront a marital issue. While some of us are uncomfortable with the idea of voices, the reality is that you largely live your marital life while holding inside the obvious and subtle messages that you've learned from the voices of others. You have cleverly transformed these to now represent your own voice of reason. Here are the voices rattling around inside your head that I ask you to consider:

Child voice.   What messages did my parents send me, and how are they affecting my reaction? What would they tell me to do if they were frozen in the mind-set of how they used to act when I was a little girl?

It may be hard to imagine, but you've learned a lot from those little-girl years. Every time your parents touched, kissed, or fought directly affected many parts of you. There are two parts of your parents' voice that I'd like you to focus on: (1) the message they sent you about marriage through their own marital behavior (that can be scary for some), and (2) the message your father sent you through his relationship with you (did he give you the message that men are loving and gentle, tough and protective?). Identifying these areas for yourself will immediately give you great knowledge regarding what you bring to your own expectations of marriage. Who's really supposed to initiate sexual contact, who's supposed to be the cuddly one, what does a real man want from his wife? Is a gentle man a turn-on or turn-off? The little girl inside of you has a lot to say about it all.

Society voice.   Your friends, siblings, and the media all tell you what they believe you should and should not be thinking and doing in your marriage. You are bombarded with subtle as well as blatant messages of how you are to behave. These others are, in part, making up your mind about your role in and what kind of marriage you "should" have.

Home voice.   Your home is telling you daily messages about your marriage. Are your kids telling you to go out and have a nice time with Dad—"Hey, go ahead and make love in the bedroom. We'll be quiet and keep busy." They may also be telling you some very positive things about marriage ("We love it when Mommy and Daddy kiss and are nice to each other"). Your bills are telling you one thing (work, work, work, no time for a night off with your husband or a romantic vacation away), and your heart is telling you something else. Your husband is telling you many things about marriage as well. Learn to focus on what these home messages are.

Inner Voice Recognition Formula

Recognize the three voices in your head that affect your relationship with your husband.

Child voice:
  What would my childhood (my parents' messages and their own marriage model) suggest I do?

Society voice:
  What would my friends, siblings, or the media suggest I do?

Home voice:
  What would my children or home pressures suggest I do?

Insight change: Which voice do *you* want to listen to in this specific instance?

In clearly considering these voices, you'll give yourself the control to decide whether you want to act based on certain voices of others or whether you'd like to create a new voice of your own—that's what I call the insight change.

You will recognize that there are some voices you can begin to discount even though you've been adopting their opinions for some time. Conversely, there are many voices that work very well in your life, and you surely want to continue to encourage them. But now you'll have the ability to see what is really driving you and give yourself the option of how you want to feel and act in any given situation.

Ultimately, you must create your very own voice that you are fully accountable for as a culmination of thinking through these other opinions—one you are going to need to make the necessary, positive changes in your marriage. It's your marriage, and guess what? Your parents, friends, and even your kids (at least long-term) won't be living it. By identifying why you are resistant to or uncomfortable with the changes being asked of you, you can then work to develop your own unique voice that will allow you to create whatever marriage you decide on.

Now you are ready for the specific behavioral changes that will be offered in this book, everything from how many times a day to compliment your spouse to how to make sex fun and pleasurable for you as you take charge and increase the frequency. You'll be focused on creating concrete, realistically attainable goals for yourself. The Inner Voice Recognition Formula will work again and again as you become familiar with automatically thinking through your struggle using its method.

When Appreciating Your Husband Is a Turn-off: Cindy's Story

Cindy is a woman I interviewed informally for this book. She believed her husband might have been cheating although she'd never caught him and he'd never admitted to doing so. When I discussed my research findings with her, she seemed appalled. "I should be more appreciative?" Then, without discussing what appreciation even translated to, she continued with, "As a woman, and I think I speak for most, you need to know that thinking your man needs a lot of cuddling and fuzzies is kind of a turn-off."

And that's where Cindy left it. She had an immediate negative response to the appreciation picture she had formed in her head. This was a really complicated issue. It wasn't that she didn't want to do it because he wasn't nice or supportive of her. She was stating that if she forced herself to do it there would be an extremely negative impact on her ability to find her husband attractive. Seems like another one of those mysterious feelings that simply happens, it's just the way it is.

Using the Inner Voice Recognition Formula, she thought through her feelings on the subject:

Child voice. Cindy's mother was constantly criticizing her dad because he was always floating between jobs. Cindy's mom always had to find jobs to keep the family afloat. Cindy and her two brothers always felt bad for their mom and were angry at their dad for putting mom in an uncomfortable position. Cindy didn't have to judge her parents one way or the other. She didn't have to say that her mom was wrong to criticize Dad or that Dad really wasn't as bad a character as the family had painted him. What she did have to realize was that her mom was clearly not appreciative and sent the message to Cindy countless times that she had better find a man who puts food on the table and allows her to be a proper mother—something Cindy's dad didn't do in her mom's opinion. Cindy was raised to have a condescending view of her disorganized, unsuccessful dad and she formed an image of a husband as a capable wage earner who knew his way around the financial world. This image was one of doing the "right thing" and providing for one's family, an exact sentence Cindy heard her mother shout at her dad countless times.

When Cindy heard appreciation, she heard her parents, specifically her mother, telling her father how he fell short and wasn't a real man in her eyes. Cindy clearly saw the idea of giving appreciation as condescending to the real man who should never need or want such things. He should be capable on his own with no help from anyone.

Society voice.   Cindy's friends generally complained about their husbands. Years ago the complaints started as funny idiosyncratic stories about their husbands, but as time marched on and two out of three of her best friends were divorcing, true love became a fantasy term for fairy tales. After consideration, she decided that her social circle didn't support any idea of appreciation and as far as the media were concerned, the ads that spoke to her reflected men whom she saw as not looking for a compliment. She'd see these men advertise a confident, powerful male beyond any need for a woman to boost his ego.

Home voice.   Cindy realized that her kids would love to see her offer her husband some appreciation. She knew how much they enjoyed seeing Dad do kind things for her, whether it was a hug, a kiss, or any playful gesture. She felt confident that her home voice would greatly support her appreciation of her husband. She didn't think any kind of home pressures stood in the way of her being more appreciative of her husband. She wasn't sure what her husband might tell her. She had previously convinced herself that he would find her condescending if she openly appreciated him.

Insight change.   The moment of truth—why was Cindy so resistant to the idea of appreciating? Cindy began to see that she was acting in a way that spoke to her childhood home environment. Now she remembered certain women she'd met through her kids' school that she felt uncomfortable around. She recalled that they

Inner Voice Recognition Formula: Cindy

Cindy felt little appreciation toward her husband.

Child voice:

> Her mom put her dad down for always falling short of her goals. Her dad had to work harder.

> Result: Don't appreciate your husband; keep pushing him to work hard and be a success.

Society voice:

> Her girlfriends complained about their husbands. The media showed men as strong with little need for appreciation.

> Result: Emphasize the negatives of your husband; he should be strong enough not to need appreciation.

Home voice:

> The kids would love to see Cindy offer her husband appreciation and disliked when Cindy put their dad down in any way. Home pressures didn't stand in the way of appreciation.

> Result: Give your husband lots of hugs and kisses, and warm gestures to show your appreciation.

Insight change: Her Inner Voice Recognition Formula activated the child and society voices. Cindy had to reset to a new inner voice that activated and focused fully on she did home voice.

were pretty upbeat about their husbands. Although at the time she had found reasons not to create enduring friendships with those women (not her type, not enough time), she now wondered whether she was really shying away from them in part because they spoke of their husbands in a way that didn't support her parents' voice. So instead she surrounded herself with girlfriends who thought very much like she did on the subject.

The Voices You Can Change Right Now

There are many differences between child, society, and home voices. Most notably, your child voice has been around a longer time and began when you were a young, malleable person ready to absorb the voices of those most special to you. Often, as we see in Cindy's case, we end up using that voice to direct our path and find others and situations that feed that original voice. It's comforting to find that your feelings and instinctual reactions are shared by others, so we're great at finding those people.

As you consider your society and home voices, consider whether you have developed them based upon the original child voice. Cindy did with her friends. This can even explain your personal relationship with the media. Do you enjoy television shows, movies, and magazine articles about couples who argue and yell a lot, have no time for their spouses, and poke fun at couples who have a great sex life? Is it possible that there is a part of you that finds these media more interesting than others that reflect genuine work to improve a marriage? Be willing to be boldly honest with yourself and see if you've surrounded yourself with the negative messages of marriage, unaware that they have been supporting your child voice.

Perhaps you've also done this with your home voice. We teach our children how a marriage works. Are you building a home that supports a loving, appreciative marriage or one that falls short? Have you taught your children the importance of their parents having time alone so that they can be better partners, which will in turn be a great benefit to your children? Look at your home voice and consider whether you've allowed it, in part, to become a voice that supports your child voice.

The most important difference between your child voice and your society and home voices is that you can create change in the latter two. Your childhood is over and done with, and even though you can understand its impact better and make necessary changes in your life based on that impact, you can't literally go back and change it. You can change your society, though—you can find friends who support your new voice directed at appreciating and being thoughtful toward your husband. You can bring that discussion into the conversations with your present friends. You can stop sharing negative things about your husband that cause your friends to egg you on and build your anger. You can change the shows you watch to more uplifting themes. The media present plenty of different images for every walk of life.

Cindy didn't really know what appreciation looked like. But she started by thinking about the one voice that supported the idea of appreciating her man: her kids. "What would that voice tell me to do?" she asked herself, and she made a quick list of things that she thought her kids would love to see. She committed to doing them regardless of whether the kids were there to see them.

Cindy kept in touch with me for only a short while, long enough to share that she was making changes and at first had to repeatedly remind herself not to get hooked into her parents' voice. Eventually she began to enjoy her new voice. "My husband has been shocked and it has made a change in him." She had discovered that her new-found appreciation did allow him to feel that she really liked him, and it opened a window for him to feel more comfortable with giving to her.

The men in my research would continuously describe a turning point in their marriage when they stopped trying to relate to their wives. Again, without blaming their wives, these men felt that they primarily heard criticism about whatever they shared, whether it was how they dealt with a business, family, or parenting matter. They felt they were being corrected and found themselves sharing less and less. Cindy was struck by how much more her husband was relating to her after she focused more on what he was doing right instead of her old voice that, like her mother, was adept at pointing out what he was doing wrong.

When You Have No Compassion for
Your Husband: Lisa's Story

Lisa contacted me with her husband's consent after he had completed the questionnaire. I'm pretty sure that her primary goal was to find out which questionnaire he chose to fill out, but she quickly learned that my research was anonymous so I didn't have names attached to the materials. She agreed to be another female voice to discuss her situation and possibly put the formula into action.

Lisa admitted that she was not a compassionate person. It took me by surprise that a person would be so comfortable characterizing herself that way. She defended herself by explaining how well she cared for her home. Organized and educated, she felt confident she was offering her children a good upbringing. She was not willing to say she was not compassionate with regard to her kids. That was a fascinating difference. She could speak comfortably about not being compassionate toward her husband but felt strongly otherwise as it related to her kids. She'd spend time shuttling them everywhere with the precision of a Fortune 500 CEO and make sure there was time to connect and have fun with them as well.

Lisa was a homemaker and her husband, Geoffrey, was the bread-winner. She took her job so seriously that she simply had no time for him. Listening to her daily schedule, I had no doubt she was right. She was candid about her husband's complaints that she was "cold" to him, and attributed it to the maintenance of her motherhood. Her husband would have to understand. "After all, he's not a kid. He can wait and learn that he can't have what he wants when he wants it. And he should want his kids to have a great mom." Lisa made a great deal of sense, but I reminded her that her original purpose of her contacting me was to find out which questionnaire her husband had completed.

Lisa agreed to work within the Inner Voice Recognition Formula and share her discoveries with me.

Child voice.   Lisa's mom passed away tragically in a car accident when Lisa was eleven. This left her dad with her older sister, Lisa, and her twin brother. Lisa thought the world of her father. As she became an adult her reverence for him grew as she realized what an outstanding father he was to his kids. He worked tirelessly not to miss a beat. He made sure he picked up the slack and never made his kids feel like they lacked a mom. He became Mom and Dad, and even though there was sadness, he created a lifestyle for them that made them feel very well cared for.

Lisa went on about how selfless her dad was and still is. She joked that everyone had to think for months about what to get him for his birthday because there was nothing they could get him. They'd usually end up sending a meaningful card with a meaningless tie to mark the occasion. He would not let them spend any real money on him. He strongly preferred that they spend it on themselves. He wouldn't call them for a favor that might take them away from their kids or spouses for even an hour.

Dad sounded like a remarkable man. Who would've guessed his incredible selflessness might hold the key to Lisa's marital downfall? Was there anything in her father's voice about her being thoughtful and loving toward her husband? If she'd ask him today, he'd emphatically insist on her loving him to no end. But the voice frozen when Lisa was young was "Don't give to Dad. There's really nothing you can do for Dad except take good care of yourself." Dad's happiness and greatest joy came through seeing his kids excel and find happiness in life. Lisa took that message and parlayed it into her own voice: men don't need kindness and compassion. That got translated into "He doesn't/shouldn't want it."

Obviously, we're not going to beat up her dad for not being needy enough or allowing his kids to feel greater responsibility for giving to him. That's why we don't have to use the formula to judge our parents, only to discover the impact their perspectives had on us.

Society voice.   When I brought up this voice, Lisa immediately put her thoughts toward her two dearest friends, her older sister and twin brother. After their mom's passing they'd become an inseparable team, and even though her older sister would leave the house two years after the tragic turn of events, they remained closer than ever. Lisa was so close to her siblings that they all lived within a one-hour drive of each other. Their families spent time together regularly and had little need for other close friendships. This voice spoke the same as her childhood one. They all loved Dad to pieces, and both her brother and sister were model parents, one having won the parent of the year award in his son's school.

Home voice.   When Lisa really considered what her home was telling her, she came up with a resounding voice to keep doing what she was doing. Although she assumed her kids would like it if she was compassionate toward their father, they were consumed with school and activities. Clearly, they were very dependent on Mom and had a lot of needs and required a lot of support. Lisa joked that maybe they'd developed that depending over the years but again reminded me that kids are only young once and as parents we can never go back and correct things. Somehow, that theory slipped her mind regarding her marriage. Naturally, she'd say that her marriage would still be there years from now—but maybe not, she thought, if her husband was cheating.

Insight change.   Lisa heard the voices. All three spoke loudly to one single message that controlled her belief system. Was she willing to continue to adopt these voices as her own? She had never thought it all through but recognized that her marriage was way off kilter and that it just wasn't working. We spent time to understand that she wasn't wrong—that seemed important to her. But her husband had stopped sending messages to her about his unhappiness so long ago that she was worried it was too late.

Inner Voice Recognition Formula: Lisa

Lisa reserved her compassion for her kids, not her husband.

Child voice:

She had a selfless dad who avoided receiving from his kids.

Result: Put all your energies into your kids, not your husband. Your husband doesn't deserve compassion for doing his job.

Society voice:

She was close to siblings who felt the same way as her child voice.

Result: Give more of your support to your kids than to your husband.

Home voice:

Her kids were trained to receive enormous attention and support from their parents.

Result: Keep giving to your kids.

Insight change: Lisa's Inner Voice Recognition Formula activated all three of her voices, resulting in complete attention and focus on her children while purposely not focusing on her husband. She had to develop a new voice, one that put importance on compassion toward her husband. She understood that she could not rely on her inner voice tracking system.

Interestingly, Lisa turned toward her dad, discussed the Inner Voice Recognition Formula with him, and got his approval. Going a step further, he brought his three kids together and discussed Lisa's insights so as to possibly help them all. I grew to have real respect for this unusual man. He even went so far as to tell them he'd been wanting to go on a cruise and would love it if everyone could go together around his birthday and he'd let them pay for themselves. Actually, he only let them pay for the adults and insisted on paying for his grandkids and himself, but this was still a great deal of progress. Lisa's dad gave her the permission she sought in order to counter the voice of her childhood father.

For Lisa, becoming compassionate and focusing on more thoughtful gestures toward her husband would require a major overhaul. It wasn't easy, because she had created a life that left her overscheduled and overtired. But with some time and by consistently returning to the formula to offer her insight and allow her to be the real compassionate person she now felt she wanted to be, she was confident she'd get there.

When He Doesn't Deserve Anything: Linda's Story

Linda was stuck. Her husband was a partner in a very successful business. The problem was that the other three partners were her husband's father, brother, and sister. After a few good years, Linda began to hate her husband's family. She felt that no matter what the situation was, her husband sided with them. He was unwilling to hear the slightest issue she might have with his family. She began to wonder if they were taking more money out of the business than her husband. Even though she and her husband lived well, it seemed that her sister-in-law lived much better. She resented the fact that her husband seemed to work harder than the others. He kept telling her that his family was generous and they all trusted one another.

These discussions overtook her marriage, and it wasn't long before Linda and her husband seemed to be on opposite teams and were sinking fast. When Linda read part of my manuscript (I asked some wives of the men I interviewed to review it for me), she contacted me with her dilemma. She couldn't imagine doing anything kind for her husband at the point where she was. She didn't think he deserved anything and surely wasn't going to "give in" to what she believed was his fault. However, she readily admitted that she loved him and their two children very much.

"It looks very rosy on the outside but on the inside it's all falling apart," she told me.

She used the formula to better understand herself and work on making changes.

Child voice.   Linda had suffered the terrible tragedy of losing her father to a murder when he was killed during a robbery of the store he and his brother owned. She was seven at the time of her loss and remembered all the details of the police officer coming to her home and her mother's hysterical wailing. Her grandmother moved in and remained with them for many years until she died the year before Linda went to college.

Needless to say, life changed drastically. Unfortunately, her father's brother, who was the partner in the store, did not do the right thing after her father's death. Linda's uncle claimed there was no provision for her father's death and the business didn't have the money to give anything to Linda's mom. The uncle ended up a fabulously wealthy man and his children were allowed to become partners in the store. Linda grew up with this painful reminder of her dad's passing as her mother had to find low-paying menial jobs in the midst of her grief. The uncle whom Linda once loved and her cousins were quickly seen as evil people and she wasn't allowed to see them even though they lived blocks away and the family used to be together every weekend before her father's death. Linda remembered the screaming that went on at times when her father's mother tried to make peace and Linda's mom confronted her angrily.

Society voice.   Linda was largely surrounded by her husband's family. Her kids had grown up used to being in each other's homes and Linda never wanted to stand in the way of family. Her husband's family was so well-known in the community that she felt it impossible to make new friends of her own. She was always part of her husband's family and could never get away from it. They had talked to her at times about her feelings and how they didn't want to stand in the way of her marriage, but Linda felt they were saying it because they had to.

Home voice.   Her children loved the big family and the fun everyone had together. They would be happy to see their mom take more part in these events and for her to love their father more. Her home was well organized and she had a live-in nanny. She had a lot of flexibility in her day and built her time around her children's needs.

Linda had always thought that her past would cause her to want a big family, and she originally was very excited to be marrying into a large, close-knit clan. But she didn't recognize her child voice that contained her mom's understandable anger at her husband's family. Linda could only now appreciate how similar her feelings were to her mother's. Without this insight, she was viewing everything her husband's family did as some personal assault. When she calmly considered them, she could see that the sum of their parts was pretty good. But the fire in her from the anger of her past never let her be anything but upset at her husband and his family.

Recognizing this gave her an immediate ability to take a deep breath and feel lighter. She looked to place her society and home voices in the forefront of her thoughts and reactions. Her husband's family seemed to want her to be happy and never put her down or purposely excluded her. Her children would be delighted to have their mom happy and not arguing with Dad about his family. Linda might only now be able to really get the big, loving family she'd been missing since she was seven years old.

Inner Voice Recognition Formula: Linda

Linda hated her husband's family and felt her husband deserved nothing from her.

Child voice:

> Her dad was murdered when she was seven. Her dad's brother was his partner in the store but gave no money or part of the

store to Linda's mom. They financially struggled and Mom hated her deceased husband's family.

Result: Linda could not trust her husband's family. She had immense anger toward her husband for being so closely involved with them.

Society voice:

Linda had difficulty finding relationships outside of her husband's family. The community knew them well, and she felt she couldn't find any other identity. His family would have been only too happy for her to be kind to her husband.

Result: Linda felt she should be kind and appreciative of her husband, but since it was his family making her feel this way, she resisted.

Home voice:

Her children loved her husband's family and anytime Mom and Dad were loving toward each other.

Result: Linda felt she should be kind and loving toward her husband.

Insight change: Linda learned that her anger was her child voice speaking for her mother. Perhaps her mother had valid reasons for her anger, but Linda no longer wanted to follow that voice in interacting with her husband. She wanted to use her society and home voices to learn to be more at peace and appreciative of her husband and his family.

Even if you feel you have little or no resistance to any of the suggestions in this book, use the Inner Voice Recognition Formula to decipher your own voices anyway. None of us is perfect nor did we receive perfect messages along the way. Sometimes you may not even realize that something makes you uncomfortable until you put it into the formula. Then you will be encouraged to work on each area as you clarify how you can sharpen your own internal messages and make your voices work for you.

Step Five: Emotional Giving

In order to help you with making changes, take the time to use the Inner Voice Recognition Formula for yourself. Since we've learned that appreciating and caring gestures are so important to your marriage, regardless of whether you feel comfortable or not with these concepts, get a deeper understanding of yourself in these areas. See what voices you're activating and which ones you'd like to activate more often.

APPRECIATION

Child voice

- What did my childhood say about a wife appreciating her husband?
- Did my mother show a lot of appreciation to my father?
- Was I shown appreciation for who I was as a child?

Society voice

- Do my friends and siblings appreciate their husbands?
- What messages do the media I seek out offer me about appreciation of my husband?

Home voice

- How do my children feel when I am appreciative to my husband?
- Is my home run in such a way that it gives me the best opportunity to offer my husband appreciation?

Insight change

Which voices would I prefer to be using and how can I remind myself to be more in touch with them?

WARM AND THOUGHTFUL GESTURES

Child voice

- What did my childhood say about a wife offering warm and thoughtful gestures to her husband?

- Did my mother show a lot of warm and thoughtful gestures to my father?

- Was I offered many warm and thoughtful gestures as a child?

Society voice

- Do my friends and siblings show their husbands a lot of warm and thoughtful gestures?

- What messages do the media I seek out give me about offering my husband many warm and thoughtful gestures?

Home voice

- How do my children react when I am thoughtful and warm to my husband?

- Is my home running in such a way that it gives us the best opportunity to show and receive thoughtfulness and warmth from each other?

Insight change

Which voices would I prefer to be using and how can I remind myself to be more in touch with them?

When Your Sex Life Is Unfulfilling

The next three stories relate to the very important question of sex in your marriage.

Katheryne's Story: Businesswoman First, Sex Partner Last

Katheryne had been married for eight years. She and her husband had two kids, ages five and six, and owned a successful real estate company, but in spite of the all the joys they shared her husband had been complaining for years that she wasn't into sex. Katheryne claimed all her husband could think about was sex. She hated the adolescent innuendos and his constant groping. She ultimately found herself resenting her husband, who in her opinion did not try to "make love" and had no idea how to really please a woman. She was tired and overwhelmed with her career and parenting responsibilities.

Child voice.   It wasn't until Katheryne was in college that she learned from her mom that her dad had cheated. Apparently, he had had a mistress for a long time and although Katheryne hadn't known, she wasn't surprised when she found out. Her parents fought a lot and there weren't many displays of affection between them that she could remember. She felt her father was pretty condescending to her mother and said that was why her mom started drinking. She had great sympathy for her mom because she was treated poorly and with little respect. This was the primary reason that Katheryne rose to the head of her class in school, then in college, and finally in the local women's career organization. She was determined not to be like her mom: stuck without an education or self-esteem. She was not some damsel in distress to be saved by a man and then tossed aside. That's why she was fifty-fifty partners in everything with her husband, and she always made sure that everything was legally scripted to show that they were full partners.

Her dad's lack of respect for her mom did ultimately have some positive affect on Katheryne. It caused her to be hyperfocused on not depending on her man. At the same time, her dad's disrespect for her mom wreaked havoc on her sex life. Her dad demeaned her mom in many ways, the least of which was considering her only valuable as a sex object. In fact, Dad was proud of the *Playboy* magazines around the house and boasted that he'd pass them on to his son, Katheryne's older brother by a year, when he turned twelve. Her whole childhood was filled with stories about cheap women, all the conquests of her brother and his friends.

Katheryne's anger about men demeaning women was deep rooted within her physical self. She felt that men saw women as sexual conquests and, once they had a woman, she was nothing more than an animal. It wasn't surprising that Katheryne was a virgin until her last year of college and she had refused countless offers to have sex along the way. She lost many an interested man due to her only-when-I-can-trust-you-can-we-go-further attitude. When she married, she saw herself as a businesswoman first, a parent second, a good friend third—never as a sex object, or a sex partner for that matter.

Katheryne disliked sex and she certainly did nothing to make it better. There was only "sex" to her: the conquest of a man taking over a woman and reducing her to a mere physical object. Once she had her two kids and no plans for more, sex became distasteful for her. She could give it to her husband as a wifely duty now and then. If he'd leave her alone about it, she'd make sure he'd get it once a week or two. That wasn't too bad in her opinion. So the fact that her husband kept after her for sex and couldn't hug her without suggesting it in crude ways drove her crazy. One time at work he squeezed her breast when they were alone in the office and she slapped him. She couldn't believe her reaction but clearly felt that she was justified; after all of her hard work through life, she wasn't about to allow her work space to identify her as sex object.

Society voice.   Katheryne was surrounded by women who enjoyed sex and would joke about how prudish Katheryne was. Katheryne would dismiss their comments by explaining how they weren't as accomplished in their careers as she was so they had to pump themselves up in another way: claiming to be sexual. In the past, based on her childhood voices, she found this pathetic. But now she could see that these girlfriends had legitimate accomplishments—whether as parents, wage earners, or in community service—even though they all made significantly less money than she did.

Her society voice told her sex was fun and the only complaints related to being too tired and never having enough energy for it. Her friends would discuss different things they'd do to make it happen and at times would even be graphic about things that worked for them sexually. It was at those moments especially that Katheryne would become uncomfortable and feel like a prude. This voice in Katheryne's life was a positive one that told her it was normal for women her age to want lovemaking and to make it enjoyable.

Home voice.   Katheryne was not surprised when she realized that her kids were not making it easier for her to have sex. Her bedroom had an open-door policy and whether they were getting a cup of water or just sharing a funny thought, her two kids were in and out of her bedroom at night until everyone fell asleep. The revolving door never bothered Katheryne. Quite the opposite. She was doing something great for her kids, allowing them to connect with her at any time before the house settled down completely and everyone was in bed. She thought it was childish of her husband to complain that they didn't have enough private time. After all, they worked together all day and often were alone discussing business. So creating the time and privacy to make love was not something her children would likely support.

However, Katheryne did recognize that she probably developed that voice herself because she never tried to institute a space that was private enough for her and her husband. So her children were really following her own voice, which she realized was mired in her childhood. She passed her child voice to her own children, and they reinforced it in her home voice. Still, under any circumstances, she recognized the voice of her home would be more of an impediment to great sex than an aid.

> ### Inner Voice Recognition Formula: Katheryne
>
> Katheryne was a proud businesswoman who felt it somewhat beneath her to be into sex.
>
> Child voice:
> > Her dad cheated on her mom and was condescending toward her. He loved *Playboy* magazine. Women were demeaned and often reduced to mere physical objects.
> >
> > Result: Found sexuality demeaning, disliked sex.
>
> Society voice:
> > Friends enjoyed sex and called Katheryne prudish.
> >
> > Result: Sex can be fun, but Katheryne explained this away by saying that these women weren't as accomplished as she was so they had to find other ways to feel good about themselves, and sex was one of them.
>
> Home voice:
> > Open-door bedroom policy meant her kids were in and out of the room all night.
> >
> > Result: No chance for privacy; no space for intimacy.
>
> Insight change: Katheryne's Inner Voice Recognition Formula made her realize how her dad and brother had poisoned her view of sex. She was a take-charge person everywhere else—except here. She would create a new voice based on her society voice, which gave her permission to indulge in the self-pleasure and intimacy of sex.

Insight change.   After considering her three voices, Katheryne could understand how her child voice, created by her dad and brother, was controlling her ability to make love with her husband. For the first time, she considered that sex had been poisoned for her because it was treated in such demeaning terms. And her mother represented womanhood as not having much more than sex to give, another negative voice inside Katheryne that caused her to run from her husband. She even chuckled when she realized that everywhere else in her life she was a take-charge person: at work, as a parent. She had no problem talking to her husband as an equal and even promoting her opinion. But when it came to sex, she lay there and quietly waited for her husband to do it all. She couldn't participate, let alone lead. This was the voice of her mother and father who taught her through their modeling that sex was about pleasing the man who was basically using the woman for his own satisfaction.

Now Katheryne felt she could use this information to help her create a new voice. She felt she had the support of her own society, that is, the support of her friends who at times openly talked positively about their sexuality. She decided to apply her educational abilities to her bedroom life and purchased different books about sexuality, making love, and her womanhood. She'd no longer give in to her husband doing his thing but would find a way to make it their thing. She was convinced that he'd hate the idea of her leading or demanding certain things in bed and was shocked when he was quite excited about her changes. He was more than comfortable with her dictating positions that gave her a greater sense of control during lovemaking. He was happy to learn which phrases she liked to hear him say during their lovemaking (and to stay away from the ones she didn't like because they spoke solely to her physicality). He was willing to stop the innuendos and adolescent remarks and promised never to touch her at the office. He was happy because his wife was showing him how to please her and learning to enjoy sex with him. It meant more frequent sex and his feeling that she appreciated him and was attracted to him. Katheryne was surprised to learn that her husband had been feeling unattractive for some time; he felt like a heel for "forcing" her to have sex with him. It was an immediate change for both Katheryne and her husband once she decided to release herself from the voice of her parents and choose a new voice supported by her society that spoke to her truer opinions about herself.

Lorna's Story: Maybe Sex after a Few Drinks

Lorna had been rather sexual her whole life. At least that's the way she saw herself. The problem was, her sex life with her husband was up and down. She blamed it on him. He wasn't sexy, kissed much too roughly, and all he could ever think about was sex. But when she really considered him, she recognized that he was a very supportive man who loved her dearly. Sure, he had his deficits and wasn't that exciting a guy—in fact, he was methodical and bland—but there really wasn't a clear reason why she should be turned off to sex at times in her married life.

Sex had become something she enjoyed now and then, usually after she'd had a round or two of drinks. Otherwise, she did it to please her husband, and most of the time she just couldn't. Her husband stopped trying to initiate a long time ago. She genuinely felt bad because she had been so sexual for so long and now had just lost it. She even visited her gynecologist, insisting that during her last birth, a C-section, something internal must've been severed that led to this sexless feeling. By the time Lorna used the Inner Voice Recognition Formula she had been turned off to sex for a couple of years.

> *Child voice.* Lorna felt her parents were quite loving toward each other and they loved her very much as well. But she told me that she had some uncomfortable moments with her older stepbrothers. I explained to her that the voice of her parents extended to any voice in her childhood home that spoke loudly to her. Her parents had both been married before and she was the only child from their second marriage. She had an older step-sister and two older stepbrothers, three and five years older, who had played ugly "games" with her when she was between the

ages of seven and ten. These games consisted primarily of her doing sexual things to them. It stopped when her brothers went away to boarding school. She never told a soul. By the time she was thirteen, she was promiscuous, although she never thought of herself in this way, and did things she'd be horrified about if her own daughter were to do them.

Society voice.   All of her friends complained about their husbands. She couldn't think of one who really loved being married. But all of them seemed to get to someplace that held a steadiness she herself didn't feel. She didn't talk about sex with her friends—quite the contrary. Because of her past she avoided the whole topic, never wanting to be put into a position where she might slip and share the abuse she suffered as a girl. She believed that as much as her friends complained about their husbands, they had a pretty good sex life and seemed content.

Home voice.   Lorna admitted to herself that her home was in disarray. She never claimed to be a good homemaker, and this bothered her because she felt that it was her job. She felt that since her husband was the sole earner of the family, she was largely responsible for the care of the kids and home. Yet she felt like a failure. Her home was not organized and her kids led unstructured lives. She had an older daughter from her first marriage who was somewhat independent but still needed homework reviewed, and two younger ones who seemed to need everything. They did their homework at different times every day, because each child was involved in after-school activities. Dinner was thrown together, as was bath time. Lorna never felt caught up with laundry and food shopping. By the time she finished her mom duties she was so exhausted that she barely had enough strength to brush her teeth, let alone have sex. She often fell asleep before her older daughter and even before one of the younger ones as well. No doubt, the voice of her home was not one that told her to love sex with her husband.

Insight change.   The Inner Voice Recognition Formula helped Lorna clearly see how the voice of her childhood was overpowering any other voice she could hear internally. She began to sense that all of the sex she had had earlier was much more about pleasing boys and men than really enjoying it and loving it herself. She recalled not having an orgasm until her mid-twenties, about ten years after the first time she had sex. Her stepbrothers' voice was an awful one, and the fact that she didn't share it with her parents because she was terrified that she'd be seen as the bad one somehow left her with a sick, valueless, out-of-control feeling. She sought control through sex, the one thing she'd been taught that boys value. She could pretend to control her world through her promiscuity.

This continued into her adulthood and her two marriages. Even when sex was often and great it was always about Lorna pleasing her man. She enjoyed it most when she initiated and controlled the environment. She realized that she was now once again in control of sex, doling it out to her husband whenever she decided.

Lorna began to reconstruct her sexuality. She wanted to find a new healthy voice that allowed her to truly connect during sex. She had to allow her husband to fully please her and make it primarily about her on some occasions. She had to stay with him and allow him to initiate and not confuse him with the ugly voices that devalued her and threatened her control.

Lorna spoke openly to her husband and requested that she take control of the lovemaking for the time being in order to help her with her issues. She was able to develop her own voice slowly but surely. She even came to realize that the past abuse she had suffered contributed to the disarray of her home. The abuse caused her to be out of control, and her house symbolized that. She called a clutter counseling home-organizing service that helped her designate a place for everything, get her kids' homework schedules synchronized, plan and post menus, and schedule time for herself.

Lorna not only regained her sexuality over time but also her sense of value and ability to create a more structured, warm home life.

Inner Voice Recognition Formula: Lorna

Lorna's childhood abuse sabotaged her marriage.

Child voice:

> Her parents were loving to each other but her stepsiblings played ugly games with her, compelling her to perform sexual acts on them, when she was between the ages of seven and ten.

> Result: Sex is attached to wrongdoing, guilt, and being controlled.

Society voice:

> Her friends complained about their husbands. Lorna avoided the topic of sex due to her discomfort around it.

> Result: Just settle on your marriage and don't rock the boat.

Home voice:

> Her home was in disarray.

> Result: Feelings of failure and being overwhelmed.

Insight change: Lorna's Inner Voice Recognition Formula showed her how her past abuse was controlling her intimate life, and her friends and home were not supporting any better direction. She needed to create a new voice that allowed herself pleasure and connection to her husband during sex. She planned to work with a therapist to help her not be overwhelmed by the ugly voices of the past. She'd talk to her husband about doing things that helped her feel in control of their sex life.

Alicia's Story: Sex Never Got Off to a Good Start

Before Alicia and Thomas were married their sex life had had its moments, but the day they moved in together sex came to a grinding halt. They loved each other and had sex now and then, but they usually didn't have time. They were exhausted at night, and the kids were regularly in their room. It was Alicia's second marriage, and after she had been divorced for a couple of years, her five-year-old was used to sleeping with Mom nightly. She knew she'd have to get her out of the bed when she remarried, but the guilt in her won out and her daughter was back in bed after a month of marriage to Thomas. Alicia felt that Thomas was a wonderful role model for her and all three of them had become close. Alicia's ex didn't share a good emotional relationship with her daughter, and Alicia was relieved to see how well Thomas and her daughter got along soon after the marriage.

Sex was largely reserved for when her daughter was at her dad's every other weekend. That was okay for a while, but soon life caught up, and after two more children in quick sequence, Alicia's now ten-year-old daughter was still in bed with them. With the other two kids in the picture it wasn't like there was going to be anything going on anyway.

The idea of locking the bedroom door and creating nightly privacy was so overwhelming and distasteful to Alicia that I asked her to try the Inner Voice Recognition Formula to confront this issue.

> *Child voice.* This took an interesting twist for Alicia. She remembered her parents being very sexual, so much so that Alicia grew up feeling rather lonely. She and her sister remembered putting themselves to bed while their parents were out nightly, wining and dining. Their bedroom door was always closed and her mother clearly explained that the parental bedroom was off-limits. There was limited family time in the family room, but it fell short of any real feeling of connectedness for Alicia. The one time she and her sister got the guts to sneak into their parents'

room, they discovered porn magazines and sex toys. They were embarrassed and didn't know why.

Alicia thought that her parents' voice would be calling out to her to have lots of sex and enjoy it. But she realized it was more complicated than that. The real voice of her parents, as she felt it, was their having sex at the expense of their children. Her parents' voice didn't say, "Make love and be better partners to each other and have that love overflow to your kids." It was a message of "Ignore your children and indulge yourself, whatever the expense."

Society voice.   Alicia was a schoolteacher and was around elementary school–aged kids every day. Her passion was helping children educationally and she was in the process of running for a seat on the school board. She was active in many community organizations that promoted these goals. Her friendships, social life, and spare time surrounded her genuine pursuit of school reform. Alicia didn't feel her society sent her any strong message that would lead her to a happy sexual lifestyle.

Home voice.   Needless to say, her children and home environment created an atmosphere of limited sexuality at best. Not only was there almost no privacy in the marriage, but family time was full of phone calls and chatter around community goals and children.

Insight change.   Alicia realized that she really struck out on all three voices. This was a clear call that her parents' blatant sexuality spoke loudly to how personally wrong it seemed to her. Sex equaled neglect of your children, and Alicia found her own way to avoid that. But now she could clear the way for her new voice built on her new understanding of what her marriage needed and what she and her husband deserved: a private place for each other to enjoy apart from the children and the rest of the world in a balanced way. She worked to create a different home atmosphere that naturally offered loving warmth to their children but slowly balanced that with loving warmth to her husband as well. There were many moments when her children tapped into her guilt with childlike "you don't love me" comments when the new structure was settling in. But Alicia kept her new voice ever present and stayed firm.

Inner Voice Recognition Formula: Alicia

Alicia had kids soon after marriage and was always exhausted.

Child voice:

> Her parents were so sexual that Alicia grew up feeling lonely. They were rarely home doing the Mom-and-Dad thing.

> Result: Sex and passion will make your kids lonely.

Society voice:

> She was very involved in the school board and education, and had no conversation with colleagues about marriage.

> Result: Society isn't pursuing excellence in marriage and sex.

Home voice:

> Family is defined by kids, their activities and education.

> Result: To have a fulfilling family lifestyle, put all your energy into the kids.

Insight change: Alicia's Inner Voice Recognition Formula helped her see that she was angry at her parents for their all-consuming marital love that excluded her. She wanted to develop a new voice that allowed her to love and have sex without it being at the expense of her goals for her children. She began to consider how it was really best for her children to have their parents in love. If their parents were more in love, they would have less tension and stress in the home and would perform better at school.

QUICK ACTION PROGRAM

Step Six: Sex

Even though sex was not the number one reason cheating men gave for the marital dissatisfaction they felt, 32 percent said that emotional and sexual dissatisfaction was about the same, coupled with the 8 percent who said sexual dissatisfaction was the primary issue in their marriage. Obviously, sex is an integral part of creating a loving, protected marriage.

We also learned that the sexual priority for cheating men is frequency. Consider this next list to discover where you stand on this issue and where you can begin to improve and implement some real solutions. Through your own answers to these questions, you can see where you want to start putting your energy in order to create a more physically intimate and fulfilling marriage.

1. On a scale of 1 to 10 (10 being the best), how would my husband rate our sexual relationship in terms of:
   - Frequency
   - My giving him pleasure
   - His confidence that he can give me pleasure
   - Foreplay

2. What are the best times for *me* to make love?

3. What can I do to have these times available and have the energy for making love?

4. What do I want from my husband that will heighten my sexual desire?

5. What can my husband do to increase my sexual pleasure?

6. What can my husband do to help me create a sexual atmosphere for those ideal times for sex that I listed in number 2?

7. What can I do to learn more about my body so I can better enjoy making love?

Put into effect the following actions immediately:

Week 1: Make love one more time than usual—You bring it up and initiate. For this one added lovemaking time (and at least one time each week thereafter) include:

1. At least five minutes of pleasant touching of parts of body other than sexual ones.

2. At least ten minutes of sexual foreplay before intercourse.

3. Getting close to your orgasm before intercourse begins.

4. Clitoral stimulation during intercourse.

5. The strategy that if he orgasms before you, your husband or you will continue to stimulate your clitoris so that you orgasm.

This weekly time can be planned. You can request that the two of you help get the kids to sleep at a decent hour or awake earlier than usual, before your kids.

Week 2: Lock the bedroom door.

1. After the kids are asleep, lock your bedroom door and sleep relaxed or naked (if you are uncomfortable, use the Inner Voice Recognition Formula to have an insight change—or get softer sheets).

2. Cuddle at least one time a night, if only for a minute before falling asleep.

3. Kiss each other good night on the lips.

7

Lessons from Successful Marriages

Here's a simple secret that I've shared with thousands of couples in therapy and in my seminars: successful couples accentuate the positive and diminish the negative, and failed couples accentuate the negative and diminish the positive. Failed couples tend to think that their failure is justified because of the spouse they married. They perceive successful couples as having an easy life, less stress, and fewer issues than what they've experienced. This is the number one falsehood of the failed couple. Successful couples shoulder just as many issues, whether they be financial hardships, work-related stress, childrearing issues, illnesses, and challenges with in-laws, but their system of dealing with it is an extremely different model, and that's what makes them successful.

Successful couples:

1. Recall and keep in mind the good things that are happening in the relationship

2. Realize that sometimes their spouses have an issue and therefore don't take every negative thing the spouse might do or say too personally.

Spouses in a successful marriage walk away from a fight and think, "How long am I going to be angry about this stupid issue? He's been so nice," "He's been off his game lately because he's been so stressed," "Just yesterday he did take a little extra time to be with me . . ."

Spouses in a failed marriage walk away from a fight thinking things like, "How dare he," "What's he done lately to show me any kind of love," "So what if he's stressed, so am I and isn't everyone," or "He doesn't talk to his mother that way." This spouse doesn't make the effort to excuse any behavior by recalling some of the nice things her husband did or why he may be acting this way that has nothing to do with her.

Surely I don't mean to imply that the successful couple does nothing else but excuse a fight. But a successful couple immediately diminishes the negative, gets over the fight quickly, and the offended spouse more often than not gets a sincere apology because the other spouse is so appreciative that his mistake wasn't blown up into World War III. Men commonly dig in to their point of view further when met with hostility and punitive actions. If a wife decides to stay angry at her spouse and give him the silent treatment and no sex or affection for a bit, her actions tend to do anything but get him to come around. Men tend to get angry and try to become punitive themselves when feeling punished for something they did that they've perceived as not that big a deal.

The successful couple comes back toward one other with an attitude of "I don't want to go on and on with this. Let's just apologize and please understand what bothered me." This attitude will almost always turn your husband into an appreciative spouse who can then admit to his wrongdoing as you've perceived it and even commit to giving you more of what you want in the future. The successful couple is often back in bed that night making love and deciding that they'll take some badly needed "couple time" in the next day or so to remedy the little hiccup. Successful couples are coming toward each other because they've remembered the good in the relationship even though there's some bad, as in the failed couple's relationship. They remembered that they're married and love each other. They have to make it work and why waste the time being angry? They allow themselves to feel the love that has been built in the relationship over the years—the positive—instead of keeping foremost in their minds all of the hardship they've had to struggle with.

Successful couples attack problems, not each other. They view the problem as a blameless entity and don't waste time on guilt.

The failed couple is entrenched in negativity. They don't want to give each other a single break. They're sick and tired, and not because it's gone on for years—they were sick and tired early on too. They never knew how to move through a fight, and since they held on to the fight and punished each other, they never made a resolution.

After a while there is a point at which each couple builds a history. The successful couple builds a history based largely on the happy times, the positive. The fights don't stick out so much in their memory because they weren't ongoing and punitive. The failed couple has spent years on a roller coaster and every time another fight occurs they connect the dots to every other fight that has continued to lie just under the radar.

Successful Couple Model

1. Recall and keep in the mind the good things in the relationship.

2. Don't take spouse's negativity too personally.

3. Remember that the effort for change shows the greatest love even though it may take a while to reach your ultimate marital goals.

Remember that men are emotional beings who react well to kindness and appreciation. They can say they're sorry and understand your feelings. They can do it all emotionally if given the chance, and for them that chance comes with your focusing on the positive.

One Fight, Two Ways to Manage

Let's look at two couples who have the same fight and see where each makes their move toward or away from love and success. You've been so loving to your husband, made plenty of love to him, have been thoughtful and appreciative, and today on the first day of your first vacation in years, he chose to go off fishing on a tour by himself instead of making plans with you for the day. Understandably, you feel treated quite shabbily.

If you want to be in a failed couple, you'd think about how hard you've worked to be nice to him and he hasn't appreciated it. So what if he's been so damned stressed? That's life, baby. You've been stressed with your own stuff in addition to being so nice to him during his pouty time. You say something like, "How dare you run off leaving me like some plaything that you can just have sex with and run and play by yourself. It hasn't been easy for me to do everything I've done for you while you've been so stressed. Oh, get over yourself, every man is stressed. I'm stressed. We come on this vacation, the first you've taken me on in who the hell knows how long, and you just use me."

He says, "I didn't know it was so hard for you to be there for me. You don't know what stress is. If you did you'd be much different. You think you have stress? What? Your nanny quit? Give me a break. Did you ever think this is why we haven't gone on a vacation for years?"

They have dug themselves in deep. She exploded with an outburst of emotion and love wasn't taken into account. She felt her point was totally justified, and the irony is that it *was* objectively quite valid. The manner in which she expressed herself, though, was unhealthy.

If her goal was to get her husband to understand her, apologize, and for them enjoy each other, unfortunately, she failed.

If you want to be successful, try to empathize with how hard he's worked lately and how he has become too absorbed in his own desire to destress and use this vacation for himself. Luckily, there's four more days of your time away and you can ask him to be much more sensitive to how you'd like to spend the time. You say something like, "Honey, I have been so looking forward to this trip alone with you. You've been working so hard lately and I've been trying to be there for you. You ran off today and I missed you and felt a little left behind here. I really want to plan our days so that we have some real fun together."

He will answer, "I'm sorry, I just have been working so hard and I thought this vacation would give me a little time alone to get over things [his defensive comment]. But I did that already today and you have been so great. What should we do together tomorrow?" Maybe it all sounds a little too perfect and simple, but don't fool yourself, it works. And if it doesn't, stay with it and don't give in to the failed-couple way of doing things.

Love Is in the Effort

Since you are reading this book, you have a goal in mind for how you want your relationship to improve. It may be that you want your husband to pay more attention to you, compliment you more, be more responsible with the day-to-day care of the family, be sweeter—whatever it is, you have some picture. If he commits to change in these areas, what happens when he doesn't meet your expected goal? You might grow angry, hopeless, drained, or indifferent.

What we forget is that when we truly love, all we can do is to make attempts at behaviors that will greater please our spouse. We can't necessarily reach the goal line each time and live up to our spouse's expectations. Love is not in the final result but rather in the earnest desire to please our spouse. If your husband didn't care, he wouldn't try at all.

Remember that change is the hardest thing for all of us. Making a change means we have to admit to ourselves that we're not as perfect as we think we are. There's a serious element of self-criticism when we commit to change. His willingness to make changes, whether or not spoken aloud, is proof of the love your husband has for you even if it may take a long time for him to satisfy the vision you have for your marriage. Even if you feel that you're working harder at the marriage than he is, it's critical that you recognize the effort he is putting into your relationship in order to please you.

It's okay if you lead the way as long as it causes him to make changes. Hope is what fuels change. Motivation for a man comes best from his feeling that he's made an effort and that his wife sees it and appreciates it. Hopelessness comes from a "never good enough" message that drains him and causes them to feel he can't win. That's the moment when he can easily stop trying.

Karen's Story: Why Her Husband's Effort Wasn't Enough

Karen married her high school sweetheart, Matt. Now thirty-six years old, she'd been with her husband for twenty-one years. Imagine her surprise when she felt at her wit's end with him. She'd lost her groove, as she put it. She felt their relationship might have been based on childish needs. They both came from neglectful families and practically ran into each other's arms very young when they felt they had no one else. But now they were distant, doing their own thing, hanging on to history more than any present-day vibrancy. She shared her disapproval of the way he worked until late at night, how he spent his free time with his buddies instead of with his wife and kids, how he'd rather play Internet poker at home than have dinner with her and the kids. The kids were young and whiny and he blamed her for not having a happier home when he returned after a long workday.

Matt surprised her one day when he returned home at 6 P.M. with take-out food so they could eat together and Karen wouldn't have to cook. But Karen had already cooked, so she was perplexed as to why he didn't call her to tell her in advance so she could've put her time to better use. He invited her for the first time to accompany him with his friends to a poker tournament he played in on Wednesday nights, but Karen felt he ignored her the entire time and did nothing to try to include her. She didn't know the first thing about poker or the system of play and felt like an outsider. Were her points valid? It would seem so. But she judged Matt on the final product instead of his willingness to put effort into creating something new. Matt had begun to take heed of her message, and that was the time for Karen to find ways to fit into some of those changes and applaud them.

When you applaud your husband and show your appreciation, it motivates him to be more sensitive to you and want to do more. Being loving to him is not saying that he's perfect and you don't want him to change one bit. Being loving is only saying that you're going to focus on the love between the two of you and that as long as that love translates to each of you making an effort to please each other, things can only get better and better.

To understand the situation, Karen used the Inner Voice Recognition Formula.

Child voice.   Karen's mom passed away when she was seven and her dad remarried a woman whom Karen described as Cruella De Vill shortly after. She and her three brothers left the house as early as possible, with no one staying home beyond the age of eighteen. Ironically, her dad claimed that he had stayed with his wife for the sake of the children. He'd found a way to stay as far away from his wife as possible but seemed satisfied that she'd care for his children. Unfortunately, her care for them translated into a meticulous house that represented an obsessive-compulsive cleaning disorder and structure that would put the marines to shame.

Society voice.   Karen found her friends to be as tired and lonely as she was. One dear girlfriend was already deeply involved in an extramarital affair in which Karen was often used as a front, while her other friends tolerated their husbands' hard work ethic. She was friends with other wives of her husband's work colleagues and all of them complained about the crazy work hours.

Home voice.   Karen's two kids, ages two and five, were a handful. The older one was autistic and there was no end to the therapy and stress needed to help him.

Inner Voice Recognition Formula: Karen

Any effort that Karen's husband made wasn't enough. She found valid reasons why these efforts fell far short.

Child voice:
>   Her mom passed away when Karen was young. Her dad married a woman who was very negative.

>   Result: A negative attitude toward those she loved.

Society voice:
>   Her friends were tired and lonely. One close friend was cheating on her husband.

>   Result: Marriage just existing—not good, not bad.

Home voice:
  She had two kids who loved her and their dad. One child was
  autistic and required endless therapy.

  Result: The kids would want Karen to be more positive with
  their dad, but their needs added to the stress of the marriage.

Insight change: Karen's Inner Voice Recognition Formula allowed
her to understand that the anger from her childhood and the indif-
ference of her society was causing her not to give her marriage
much of a chance. She needed to learn to activate the home voice,
the sweet voices of her children who desperately depended on the
love and union of their parents.

Insight change.   Karen felt like she struck out on the first two
voices. Her mom passing and being replaced by a neurotic,
negative woman spoke loudly to Karen and said, "Be negative,
be negative." She quickly realized that when she expressed dis-
appointment in Matt, she could've heard the very same words
come out of her stepmom's mouth. She shuddered to think that
she was taking on this mentality.

Her society voice was a tired, indifferent one. She felt her
friends were dissatisfied in their marriages and either pretended
it away or tried to solve it in unhealthy, messy ways. This voice
was surely not helping her get a positive view of marriage and
Matt. She even noticed that her facial expressions mirrored
exactly those of the women in her group.

Her kids' voice was surely the sweetest. She knew that they
loved their dad very much, and as much as he should be around
them more, he still played with them and was loving to them
when he was home. But her home voice also spoke loudly to
the hard work that was required to maintain a home with two
children, one of whom had special needs. Her kids would want

a loving environment, but the demands made by the situation created an overwhelming feeling in Karen that caused her to be angry at Matt because he didn't rescue her at times.

Karen could now begin to understand the voices. She had to develop her own new voice that didn't represent her stepmom, her need to have Matt be the father who wasn't there for her, and her anger at Matt for not rescuing her from a hard day with the children. Instead she had to find a softer voice that incorporated how much she loved Matt, that acknowledged how he too suffered and was finding his way by running away from the family. She wanted to create a voice that appreciated how Matt would try to bring her along to his world. Maybe she needed to get out with him and his friends and just watch poker, play a little, forget everything at home for the night. She needed to stop blaming Matt and realize that both of them were working hard in their own way, and if she could love Matt for attempting changes, they could start to find new ways to hold on to each other and begin making even better changes that satisfied both of them.

8

Caring for Yourself

When we are not nurtured, we cannot nurture—our marriage, our children, anyone. Jenna was an operations manager for a midsized company. She and her husband, Greg, had two children and an older child from Greg's first marriage. Although Greg was usually helpful, he often "forgot" to do the things Jenna asked of him. Even with part-time help in the house, she had endless lists of chores. To compound things, Greg's ex-wife was frequently on the phone with complaints that Jenna was expected to field relating to things she felt she couldn't possibly control, such as her husband's attendance at her stepson's football games. Jenna dealt with it all—until she didn't.

On those days, she snapped at the children and felt hopeless and angry. Usually she and Greg ended up fighting—angry fights in which they said things they didn't mean and later regretted. This had been the pattern for a while. Jenna felt that her husband was, in many ways, not unlike her children—seeking attention, negative or positive, and seeming to know when she was at her weakest. At those times he'd pick a fight or announce some new idea that he knew Jenna would oppose. Those times were becoming more frequent and her husband was getting on her nerves.

One day Jenna decided she'd had enough. She had overheard an older woman describe her own mother as someone who always "smelled good and had a smile when she saw us." Jenna realized this didn't describe her at all and that she was too tense. So she sprayed herself with Chanel No. 5 and smiled widely as she walked in the door at home. The children looked alarmed and asked what was wrong. She smiled again and continued to remind herself that she was a very lucky person, all was well. The kids reminded her of their science fair projects due that week. "You can all work on it this evening," she said. Her front began to crumble, though, when she tripped over her husband's workout shoes, left in a pile by the stairs. Although she had reminded him that morning about her stepson's important game, she saw him in front of the computer. His ex would call any minute, blaming her, again. She reminded herself that it was these small daily life stressors that built up and caused people to lose it. She breathed deeply. Her husband looked up from the computer and told her he'd invited two friends to watch the game that night. She would have to do the committee meeting alone, again. And although she knew it wasn't that big a deal and he should be able to do what he wanted in his own house, she felt like breaking down.

That was the defining moment when all the phrases came at her: "time for yourself," "overwhelmed," "multitasking," "self-soothing," "If Mom ain't happy, nobody's happy," "If you are delighted, others around you will be delighted." That was the end. She called the head of the homeowner's search committee and explained she wouldn't be able to attend the meeting. Instead she marched upstairs, took a hot bath, and realized she'd been running on empty.

She began to talk to other women about ways they coped with stress and nurtured themselves. Soon she joined a walking group, and then began exercising regularly, really enjoying the endorphin rush.

She made the house quieter and bought a small music system for her kitchen. She began to say no to unnecessary obligations both socially and at work. Jenna got a high school girl to help with the kids' homework and projects and began texting her husband reminders, which, seemed like an effective method. She invited him out to dinner and when he couldn't go, she went with a friend. She scheduled spa days once in a while and found she had creative solutions to problems on those days. Whenever she felt guilty about this time, she repeated, like a mantra, "This is good for me and good for my family."

Her husband seemed happier, and when she told her mother about these indulgences she was surprised to hear her mother encourage her, with the phrase, "Well, honey, better to spend on that than a divorce lawyer or a doctor." Her best friend said, "How can you be there for others if you aren't there for yourself?" This made sense, and although there were still challenges, Jenna found she was better able to handle them. She stopped feeling guilty and recognized that nurturing her mind, body, and spirit was not a weakness or a sign of selfishness, but a strength that enabled her to be present in her marriage, her work, and her family.

Caring for Your Physical Self

The expectations placed on you today may be greater than ever before. Pressure often builds when we are asked to do so many different things. To have time and focus in order to excel in one primary area of your life is often far less stressful than being expected to excel in multiple areas even if the actual time spent is the same.

A prescription drug benefit manager, Medco Health Solutions, estimates that 16 percent of U.S. women between twenty and forty-four, nearly one in six, currently take antidepressant medications. That's up 57 percent from just five years ago and about double the number of men taking antidepressants. Similarly, in the last four years there's been a 113 percent rise in prescription stimulants to treat adult ADD for women in the same age group—a 20 percent higher growth rate than among men in the same age group. And women are twice as likely as men to fill a prescription for potentially addictive sedatives to treat anxiety and stress.

Most men can ascribe feelings of success to themselves pretty easily. Work hard, make a good living, be nice and somewhat involved with the wife and kids—bang, knocked it out of the park (man talk for a "big success"). As women, you probably feel that there's never an end to your duties, and you may rarely allow yourself a feeling of success. Many women get caught up in everyone else they love and find little time to love themselves in the midst of it all. Some women may be waiting for others like their husbands and kids to do that loving for them. That's a good idea, but there are many husbands and children who will learn to love wife and Mom based on the messages that the woman sends out about her need for loving. When wife and Mom doesn't take proper care of herself, others tend not to as well.

This is a hard area to explore, because no one else can tell you what is proper caring for yourself. I can only tell you that focusing on your need to nurture yourself is as important as the care you give to others you love. You'll be the best wife and mom you can be only if you are healthy and caring for yourself as well. Be aware not to fall into the never-ending wife and mom trap that keeps you exhausted and feeling guilty if you do anything that seems only to benefit yourself.

It would be nice if spouses easily anticipated each other's needs, wants, and desires. Maybe you feel that since you do that for your husband, he should be able to do it for you. But one of the reasons you're good at anticipating your husband's needs is that he's probably pretty decent at letting you know about them. He may be pretty good about taking time off, spending the extra time at work to complete a task, exercising, getting tickets to the ball game to unwind, and so on. The things he may not be great at expressing are the things men report wanting their wives to spend more energy on—appreciation, kind gestures, and the like. The needs that he's not skilled at expressing to you might be the needs that you are not as skilled at offering him. Maybe there's a connection?

What Advice Would You Give to Your Friend?

So consider what you would do if you were advising a friend. What would you tell a friend who was living your life? Would you tell her that she's doing great caring for herself and there is no need to better care for herself? Or would you tell her to start doing many things that you feel would cause her to treat herself kindly?

Write down a list of things you'd tell your friend if she were living your life.

The obvious two areas to consider when making positive changes in caring for yourself are your physical and emotional needs.

Physical Needs

Deal with the most important areas first. Do you eat, sleep, and exercise properly? If you have a child, I'm willing to bet you've made sure she has three square meals a day and gets enough sleep (unless she's fighting with you on bedtime). You probably are willing to do anything to make sure she gets the right amount of exercise. What about you? What do you have to do in order to make sure you get proper meals, sleep, and exercise?

We can recognize that you can't always get enough sleep. But when you're up with a sick child, work project, or home duty, is there an end in sight? Are you making sure that after the illness or project you have a night or two off when you can get more sleep? Perhaps your husband will get up with the kids in the morning for a bit until you can catch up on some sleep?

Emotional Needs

Physical needs are easier to list and more universal than emotional needs. Consider the three emotional things that are most important for you to receive from your husband. Love? Companionship? Sex? Whatever is on your list, reflect on how exactly you'd want your husband to satisfy these needs. Think about how he could best give you love. Is it physical touching mixed with pleasant, friendly conversation? Maybe having fun together? What do you do to present a situation that allows for this? I'm not saying it's only your responsibility to make it happen, but if you want more from your relationship, you're smart to create situations that allow for it. Do you have the time and space with your husband to have fun, touch lovingly, have uninterrupted friendly conversations? If not, why not?

What would you say if you were talking to a friend who presented the same issues? Wouldn't you tell her in a heartbeat to take control and get a babysitter so your husband can take you out, get some rest so the two of you can have some fun, plan a vacation even though it won't be exactly where you wanted to go because money is tight at the moment? Getting your own needs met takes a lot more than verbalizing them. Create a life environment that invites getting those needs met.

Sometimes we think the little things don't make that big of a difference. I'm all about major change and deep insight into ourselves. But I've learned that often, just ten minutes of quiet can go a very long way toward bringing some calm into our day. One hot bath won't make the difference, but it sure does make a start. The mind can feed itself when it has space, and it becomes clever and more creative the more space it has.

Peace, Tranquillity, Calm, Nurturing

What comes to mind when you think of these terms? Create a visual image. What steps do you need to take to incorporate more of these elements into your life? Consider these ideas:

1. Go to the woods. Henry David Thoreau noted, "Most men lead lives of quiet desperation." He went to the woods. You can take a simple walk. Notice the birds, breathe deeply. Studies have shown that regular exercise can be more effective than antidepressants. However, if you need antidepressants, please stay on them and use activity to supplement.

2. Write down what you loved to do in childhood. Chances are you will still enjoy those things and can incorporate them into your life now.

3. Levity—humor, lightness, laughter. These are linked to anti-cancer defenses. Dr. Mehmet Oz notes the importance of these aspects of living for antiaging effects and good health. Rent funny videos, do fun things by yourself and as a couple just for the sake of enjoying them. Develop a sense of humor by watching various comics and their styles. Cultivate funny friends. Make a play date: call and invite your funniest friend to brunch. The neuroscientist Lee Berk says laughter can make you healthier. It can lower blood pressure, cut stress hormone levels, reduce pain, relax muscles, boost immunity, and pump you full of endorphins.

4. Surround yourself with light. In addition to lighthearted people, surround yourself with lighter images. Take a vacation from the news and get rid of visual negativity. Look around your house and donate or sell things that bother you. Put your lights on dimmers. Open the blinds at times. Some doctors recommend ten minutes daily in the sun.

5. Breathe: Practice yoga, either by following DVDs or by going to yoga classes.

6. Water: the creative person SARK (Susan Ariel Rainbow Kennedy) recommends that when children are crabby, place them in water. It's good advice for adults too. Whether it's a warm bath, the ocean, your pool, or a friend's or a community pool, water is relaxing. Look to the relaxing properties of water wherever you like it.

7. Have a snack time: blood pressure drops when you wait too long to eat between meals, causing cravings and overindulging. "The biggest cause of overeating is undereating," says Katherine Tallmadge, RD, a Washington, D.C., nutritionist. Ask your doctor or nutritionist about eating for good feeling.

8. Soft clothes: how much of your wardrobe is comfortable and nurturing? Do you spend too much time in uncomfortable shoes and clothing? Fight back and give your body the feeling that you love it. You probably would do this for children and others you love. Love yourself enough to do it for you.

9. Bed: we spend a third of our lives in bed. I'm always interested in how couples treat the place they spend the most time together. It's a litmus test—when people are cheap and uncomfortable with their bed, they generally are not nurturing themselves or each other enough. Mattresses need to be replaced regularly. Is yours supporting you well? Is it a pleasure to sleep in? Do you awake refreshed? Consider getting soft, soothing sheets and a new collection of pillows.

10. *Gevonden*: our Dutch friends Henny and Marriette are two of the calmest people I know. They live a short bike ride from the heart of Amsterdam, and their lives are uncluttered, filled with what the Dutch call *gevonden*, which translates roughly to "small pleasures." These small pleasures are unique to the individual but provide the daily enjoyments that make life sweet. Rather than stress and wait (for the Vacation or the Big Night Out) to enjoy life, the Dutch take the time to savor personal enjoyments. An espresso sipped slowly as opposed to being grabbed in a mob at Starbucks and thrown back into the gullet on the way out to catch the train, a square of excellent dark chocolate, a midnight walk to a pub on a cool night—these are the good things. We feel good when our lives are punctuated with *gevonden*, better able to appreciate our spouses and ourselves.

11. Give yourself the gift of a day off. For one full day (or even a half day), give yourself permission to do exactly what you want to do and only that. No errands, nothing for the family. Plan the day, enlist family to help with the kids, or make other arrangements.

12. Grow your brain. Children do it daily. Learning something new (or doing crosswords or sudoku) is like mental gymnastics. One study showed that after just two weeks of memory exercises and puzzles, participants performed significantly better on oral exams and their brains actually used less energy while thinking.

13. Go on vacation. Research shows you've got to get away at least once a year. A large study found that women who didn't take a break were seven times more likely to have a heart attack than those who took two or more breaks a year. Stress control is crucial to heart health. Even if funds are an issue, consider just one or two nights away, or an economical vacation like camping in a national park or nearby scenic spot. Explore options on the Internet or discuss ideas with friends to find choices that please you. Just find a way to get away and turn it all off.

9

Responding to Your Husband's Love

This book has been mainly about what you can do to take the lead role and create a solid marriage. Throughout, I've been outlining a process that ensures that when you give what your husband wants, he'll give a great deal back. I've tried to put your mind at ease that he won't simply get used to getting all these new goodies from you and figure he can sit back, receive, and do nothing for you.

Now here is a crucial question. When your husband does reciprocate, how will you respond? "Come on, Gary," you're thinking, "I'd love it." I believe you. But will you do the things that will continue to motivate him to give to you, or will you do the opposite? Look, you're not going to consciously, purposefully try to discourage him from being loving. However, this doesn't mean you won't end up discouraging him. Over the years I've heard some common examples of men who try to please their wives but are shot down.

Are You Rejecting Presents?

A man buys his wife a piece of jewelry. His wife doesn't like it so much, returns it, and gets a different piece of jewelry. Sensible? Sure—that is, if you want your husband to stop purchasing jewelry for you.

Your husband buys you flowers. Your response? "Don't spend the money next time," or "Buy a plant instead because the flowers die," or "I don't like these because they have those brown thingies that stain."

A husband gets his wife a piece of jewelry, nice stuff. She likes it. But no birthday card. Or just a card that he signed, "I love you." The wife says she'd rather have no jewelry and instead a card with a meaningful handwritten message, like he used to write when they were dating.

You don't like the surprise jewelry? Maybe wear it anyway, proudly, especially if it's not an expensive piece relative to your standard. If it'll be a big, expensive gift then you do want to get something you love. Go window shopping with him. Show him what you like so he knows how best to choose. If you're still concerned, perhaps choose three different pieces you'd love to have and let him make the final decision. Find the way that he can give to you so that you'll be happy. Think about how good you feel when you've pleased him in some way. It's crucial that he have the same feeling, or else he can't win, and then he'll stop trying. Make him feel great about his giving to you on any level. Lovers should be giving to each other all the time and enjoying the process.

With this mind-set, he'll love to give to you because he loves you, because you're appreciative and kind toward him, and because it feels great for him to have the one he loves enjoy his giving so much. As you home in on the issues presented in this book, you will be creating a symbiotic relationship between your giving and his giving back. Men love to love as much as women and they enjoy being around people who love them and appreciate them. Be that person and you'll have created a wonderfully solid and protected marriage.

Cheryl's Story: Nothing for Her Birthday

Cheryl complained often that her husband hadn't gotten her anything for her birthday or anniversary for years. As much as she felt she dropped hints and was outright mad when she received nothing on these days, her husband wouldn't budge on this issue. It seeped into all parts of their couplehood. In general, Cheryl felt her husband, Richard, was unresponsive to her, completely self-focused, and took every breath of emotion she had without giving much back.

But to hear Richard talk you'd think they were discussing two completely different worlds. Richard explained that he used to get his wife presents but there was always a problem with them. Usually it wasn't as much that Cheryl didn't like the presents as that she always felt he had spent too much. They both worked hard and had saved for years to be able to feel financially stable enough to have children and purchase their own home. Whether he'd bring her jewelry or flowers, he'd get the same response: "How sweet, don't ever do it again." After a few years of that message, Richard stopped with the gifts and just gave her greeting cards. He'd get a serious one, a funny one, and an extra one just because. Cheryl found that little tradition unnecessary as well. It wasn't too long before Richard would just take her out to dinner with their two kids and have a cake at home for a small celebration.

It didn't stop there. Richard loved his wife very much but felt she would never take care of herself. She'd gained a great deal of weight and never had time to go to the gym. He offered to buy her a membership but she flatly refused it. She was so busy raising two little ones while Richard worked harder now than ever because they had decided to let Cheryl quit her job when boy number two came along. Richard wanted Cheryl to take a short vacation away with him and leave the kids with his mom, who was willing to come into town to help if they needed. But Cheryl insisted that they hadn't worked this hard and waited this long to have children in order to leave them and go off and play. There'd be plenty of time for that later. That was becoming ever so questionable, the way Richard was talking.

Upon further consideration, Cheryl was willing to take a harder look at her responsibility in this issue. What was it about her that caused her to perhaps put off her husband and his attempts to make her feel given to?

Cheryl was willing to consider her voices.

Child voice.   Cheryl described her mother as a wonderfully giving woman. She was remarkably energetic toward her eight children. She never could afford household help so she was responsible for the complete care of the home. Some of Cheryl's favorite childhood memories involved waking up at three in the morning and finding her mom ironing downstairs. Cheryl would be delighted to talk to her mom for an hour or so before returning to sleep while Mom moved on to her next task. Her mother woke in the morning cheery and would greet everyone as they piled into the kitchen to the warm scent of eggs and pancakes made with love. Mom helped with homework, got everyone to the doctor, rubbed backs with lotion after sunburns, planned every birthday and family holiday. She was a truly remarkable woman.

But like many things that look perfect, this one was not entirely what it seemed. There was some tension in Cheryl's home. Mom and Dad fought bitterly, and although they never divorced, Cheryl wasn't sure they did anyone a favor by staying together. Mom would complain about Dad never making a great living. Equally unfortunate was Mom's health, which was in peril ever since Cheryl could remember. She became diabetic and never cared for her overworked self. She passed away at sixty-two never having met Cheryl's children and suffering for years toward the end as her self-neglect settled in and took hold.

Society voice.   Cheryl and Richard lived in a child-oriented community. The families in the neighborhood regularly got together on Sundays and shared barbecues and other family events. She felt that most of the moms in her life were similar to herself, giving and wanting to be hands-on parents. All of them worked hard and didn't take elaborate vacations.

Home voice.   Cheryl knew that although her children would like their mother to be happy, they would not be happy to see her go off for days at a time and not be as involved in the daily aspects of their lives. She didn't feel that the kids would really care whether she received jewelry from Dad, but figured they'd probably be happy to see her receive presents like they did on their birthdays.

Inner Voice Recognition Formula: Cheryl

Cheryl felt her husband was unresponsive and abandoning. Her husband felt he wasn't allowed to love his wife.

Child voice:
>   Her mom was Supermom—selfless, but she complained about Cheryl's dad.

>   Result: Cheryl felt she couldn't receive, that it was more important to give.

Society voice:
>   Her community was largely about the kids, although the families did go on vacations.

>   Result: Great effort should be given to child-related activities.

Home voice:
>   The kids were happy that Mom was taking care of them. They didn't care if Mom had jewelry or not.

>   Result: Stay focused on the kids.

Insight change: Cheryl's Inner Voice Recognition Formula told her that she had turned into her mother and heard her voice loud and clear.

(*continued*)

She also admitted that her friends went on vacations and enjoyed their loving marriages. She was determined to activate her society voice and allow herself to enjoy marriage and take in its pleasures.

Insight change.   Cheryl immediately realized that she had turned into her mother. She always thought of it as a good thing but forgot that her role model did not include a happy marriage. She'd become a kind of martyr, and in that way she'd refuse overtures from her husband to give and be kind to her, instead creating an environment where she was the primary giver but then getting angry at her husband for not giving more. She was a great mom but never learned that part of being one would be to offer her children the model of a successful marriage and loving parents, as well as a mom who deserved to be cared for as much as she cared for others.

Cheryl heard her mom's voice whether she realized it or not, and it told her to avoid her husband's goodness and keep her distance while being a phenomenal mother.

Regarding her society voice, Cheryl changed her mind about her friends and decided that they would support a voice that told her to take better care of herself and allow her husband to give to her more.

Cheryl sensed that her final voice, the children and home, did not support her caring for herself and receiving love from her husband. Her kids were taught at an early age that Mom was always there and completely devoted to them. It would take a slight retraining to get them used to the idea of Dad and Mom spending time alone or away from them.

Cheryl realized that her new voice had to be much more in line with her society voice. Her friends were good mothers and yet they were able to care for themselves and be cared for by their husbands. She had to focus on not falling into the trap of being a martyr mom and pleasing her children at every turn. She needed to recognize that she deserved more than what she was allowing herself to receive. She always believed that her mother's early death was tragic because she would have loved to live longer and enjoy her grandchildren. As a kid, Cheryl would've been just fine if her mother had given to her a little less and taken care of herself a little more. In retrospect, Cheryl wished that her mother had indeed cared for herself more and had a better relationship with her dad.

Cheryl's friends were reasonable, good people and she could now use them as mentors to find her way through this specific change.

The Date Night

This suggestion was mentioned quickly before, and it is well worth revisiting. Create a regular weekly date night when you and your husband can spend a minimum of two hours together alone. Don't go out with another couple. If you must, meet them after your two hours alone for dessert or drinks. Every week use the same night as your date night so that you have a regular babysitter already set in advance that you'll have to pay for whether or not you go out. This of course will encourage you to go out regardless of how tired you may be.

The simple rules for the date night? Talk about anything but three subjects—money, business, and kids—and avoid the two most popu-lar date-night activities: dinner and a movie. Dinner is a high-pressure scenario where we're facing each other for an hour or two and now we've got to fascinate each other with conversation. How many of us can talk philosophy and discuss gossip for hours without finding our way back to the stressful topics of life? Frankly, I'm not that fascinat-ing, although lucky for me my wife is so I can always depend on her to bring up great topics and thoughtful opinions for us to share. But for most a stroll in a mall, a visit to a bookstore and a cup of coffee in its ubiquitous café, a leisurely bike ride together or listening to some jazz or music of choice at a club serves as a greater springboard for conversation and plain enjoyment. A movie is okay now and then but with regularity it can turn into a tired couple's cop-out plan, leading to little interaction about the movie's theme.

This date night has to become sacred, meaning that no one makes plans to do anything else on that night without permission from the other. Naturally, if you can't go out on your assigned date night, maintain the consistency by finding another night to go out that week. Don't let it slip away from you, because it is just too easy to stop enjoying each other.

Remember to have fun. Whatever turns you and your husband on to each other enjoying your time together is what you want to make the time to do every single week without fail. Otherwise, we lose that side of us. Life can squeeze it out of us. It's amazing to consider that the average child laughs over three hundred times per day whereas adults laugh only six to seventeen times per day. It's hard for me to believe that statistic, but whatever the case, we stopped laughing too much along the way to adulthood. The best way to get your husband to belly-laugh is to do it yourself. He'll want to date you more and more.

Don't get hung up on your husband planning the date night. It is true that most wives are typically the social calendar keeper and can get quickly tired of always having to plan the date night as well. There is nothing wrong with wanting your husband to put a little effort into a night here and there, but it's better to bring up the date night on the weekend when you're reviewing the paper with the possibility of finding an interesting weekly event that both of you can attend and asking aloud what he'd like to do the next date night. This way you can feel that you're planning it together. Once the date night becomes a regular occurrence, he'll start speaking up about what he'd like to do and will help call for tickets or make arrangements as well. Just give it time, and the more fun you have together the more he'll want to get involved.

Regular Touching

In the 1950s Harry Harlow conducted a study of newborn monkeys that revealed a powerful message about touch. Newborn monkeys were given two surrogate mothers. One model was made of wire that contained a steady supply of milk; the other was also made of wire but it was wrapped in terrycloth and was warm but lacked any source of nourishment. The infant monkeys tended to spend time with the soft yet foodless mother, even coming close to starvation as a result of their preference.

The study proved the importance of warm touch from mother to child. It also told us something about each and every one of us—we yearn to touch and be touched. Men, like women, want to feel loved through touch, and a quick loving touch is often the simplest, quickest, and most effective way to connect and provide a loving moment. Touch your husband more, stand closer to him, be freer with kisses and hugs. Create an environment where the focus to love never leaves and is easily supported with simple, loving physical gestures.

QUICK ACTION PROGRAM

Step Seven: Finding the Time to Love

We learned that the average couple spends only twelve minutes a day talking, which stacks the chances of having a loving, close relationship against us. To increase your time together, take these quick actions:

1. Establish four forty-five-minute periods a week of uninterrupted time with your husband. This is a time to relax. Consider these options:
   - Reading to each other
   - Cuddling while chatting

- Taking a leisurely walk
- Making love
- Sharing snacks and drinks out back
- Playing card and board games
- Searching online together for funny items or possible vacation destinations
- Avoiding aimless TV watching

2. Make date night each week that's:
   - The same night every week
   - Two hours minimum alone
   - Full of discussion of any topic except money, business, or kids
   - An outing other than dinner and a movie
   - Focused on fun and pleasure

3. Child management:
   - If your children aren't going to sleep on time, consider more rigorous physical activity before bedtime so that they are exhausted by bedtime.
   - Create a "night is over at nine o'clock policy." After this time, parents close the bedroom door. No test papers signed, review of homework, or allowance money should be given out after this time.

4. Beware of extracurricular activities and how tiring they can be:
   - Keep activities close to home
   - Consider putting different kids in the same activity
   - Clarify attendance expectations from the start

5. Regular touching:
   - Initiate five loving touches of your husband each day

What We've Learned about What You Can Do

One of the primary rules of marital therapy is never to make one spouse feel like it's all his or her fault. No one likes to take the blame and no one wants to work on a marriage alone. So why have I written a book aimed at women and what they can individually do to change their marriage? Simply, it works.

This book hasn't been about blame. It hasn't told you that you're at fault and therefore you alone have to carry the burden of change. I've made no excuses or justifications for cheating and never want to blame the victim. What I have done is made you a good, solid offer. You take the lead on making the suggested changes and your husband will respond in kind. I wanted to find out for you where you should focus your energy in order to create a loving, meaningful, and protected marriage.

We've read or heard about the popular book *The Secret* and the power we have as individuals to affect others. Moving forward with the suggestions made in this book can be done with the firm belief that you can make the difference. Allow yourself to visualize how you want to see your husband behaving toward you. Begin to imagine how your attempts at change will cause loving, positive improvements in the way he is with you. Show your husband how you want to be loved.

Sometimes we forget that marriages are made up of two people who *want* to be in love. Your spouse is not opposed to the idea of more love. But we fall away from the marital focus so quickly that we lose faith in our union to bring us the joy and happiness we once dreamed of. Return to seeing your husband as your ally. He wants to love and be loved by you. He wants to please you and have you think the world of him. That's why he'll recognize the changes you make, be delighted, and want to know what he can do for you.

The first time I spoke of the results of my study and some of my suggestions, I excluded men from the audience. It was part of a weeklong gathering at a conference and I decided I wanted to share it for the first time with women alone. Many men were quite nervous before the talk and approached me to try to figure out what was coming their way. For days after the talk, at least fifty husbands found me and told me, "I don't know what you did but this has been unbelievable." The mixture of joy and surprise proved that men want to enjoy their marriage and want to be close to their wives. Even more women approached me before the end of our stay to confirm for me that their husbands were loving them in ways they never thought they'd ever see. It was just a matter of a couple of days and people were reporting wonderful experiences.

My goal has been to give you clear focus on where to spend the bulk of your energy. We've learned that the following four crucial points most likely apply to your husband:

1. Appreciation and thoughtful, caring gestures mean a lot to your husband.
2. Sexual frequency is the most important issue for your husband to be sexually satisfied.
3. Staying involved with your husband's close friends, workplace, and hobbies is a great plan.

4. Make time for yourself so that you can reenergize and have the mental and emotional space to focus on your marriage.

Obviously we've covered more in this book, but just keeping these four crucial points firmly in your sights will keep you focused on the behaviors that are most likely to guide you to a wonderful marriage.

Some women are at their wit's end and are considering divorce. When you divorce, especially if you have children, you will see some serious pain, and during those moments you do not want to have any regrets. You want to be sure that you did everything you reasonably could to save your marriage and make it solid. So put the effort in the right places as I've discussed in this book and, worst-case scenario, you'll have proven that you absolutely can't make your marriage successful solely on your own efforts. You've still gained—you've gained the peace of mind of knowing you did every sensible thing you could. I also suggest marital counseling in addition to my book if your marriage is suffering (see appendix A). Again, even if it doesn't work, you need to feel deep in your soul that you really tried. Only then will you be able to get through some of the emotional struggles that may be waiting for you.

Whenever I have a wife in my office, I remind her that even though I may be challenging her, it's not to say she's the primary issue. But she is the only one present, and this I know for sure—the one in front of me can make changes. Whoever shows up in my office is the one I'm going to help. Discussing what the other person who is not present needs to do is intellectually interesting but not worth much time exploring. This is particularly true of a spouse, because I have seen that when the woman in front of me takes responsibility to change the situation, to respond differently, her husband will inevitably make similar changes. Change brings change. Often when one spouse initiates change, the other joins in. Soon he will be coming to you for change instead of you feeling like you're chasing after him.

Of course, there are no guarantees. A small percentage of men will cheat regardless of what their wives do, and then it becomes your personal choice what to do and how to manage. There are also abusive men, mentally ill men, and toxic men who feel nothing but contempt for women, and women must protect themselves from them.

But the significantly greater odds are that your husband falls into the more common category of a husband who wants to love and be in love. In a very short time frame, big changes can happen. Just stick with these suggestions and the consistency of your focus will cause a fresh message in your marriage that says, "Our marriage is a priority. We will make it loving, protected, and fun."

Will Therapy Help?

A friend I'll call Maria found out that her husband, Rolf, was cheating from a letter she found in his briefcase. Her husband had been denying anything and everything but finally had to admit to it after this evidence. When Rolf suggested counseling, Maria flatly refused. She told me, "Obviously, he needed the help. He was the one who broke our vows. Why was I going to sit and be told anything?"

Rolf did attend counseling by himself for six sessions, and when he asked Maria to attend after that point, she still refused. She told my wife and me that she hadn't heard any real remorse on her husband's part and wasn't about to be told to "understand" her husband's position and the problems in the marriage that led him to cheat.

Clearly, Maria believed that marital counseling had a certain agenda, which included explaining the cheating as a symptom of a failed marriage. Her point was valid. Even though cheating could be a symptom, it's still wrong, and the cheating deserves its own therapeutic attention without it ever being excused or explained away. But Maria's reaction caused her to miss a potential opportunity to resolve her marital problems and turn them around. It was not surprising when she later shared with me that they had divorced.

As a psychotherapist, I am surrounded by so much psychological talk that I can't imagine a world without gobs of therapy. Frankly, there was a time when I thought any therapy was better than no therapy. I've learned that I was wrong and have amended my attitude to believe that good therapy can't hurt. Marital therapy is the hardest of all because you have to imagine that by the time a couple finds their way to a marriage counselor it's usually the last straw. It's like each spouse is saying, "I don't know what to do. Everything he does bothers me, the way he eats, the way he talks, the way he sleeps, that constant breathing in and out and in and out. I can't take it anymore." Then of course the counselor is supposed to sprinkle magic pixie dust (I actually heard about some "forward-thinking" shrink who did just that) and in just fifty minutes, maybe even a double session, everyone is on better terms, and in just one hour out of a 168-hour week, all will be healed. There is no such thing as stagnating at that point in a marriage; it's either up or down. Add cheating to the mix and then you have even more hostility and unrestrained blaming going on.

Therapy is complicated from the first moment. So much so that in my practice where I see many marital patients, I will often take on the case only if the couple is willing to give me many hours in the first few weeks and at times even half and whole days. If I want to really succeed I have to set a framework that allows much of the necessary discussion to occur without worrying about the time. I've had the most wonderful experiences counseling an unhappy couple and having them prove to themselves how quickly they can turn their marriage around.

But because there is no one way of doing anything psychologically, one wonders what the real world thinks. How many couples reach out for help and how many are truly helped? There are people who'll ask marriage counselors about their rate of success as though the counselor is keeping a scorecard. I have yet to meet the counselor who responds with, "Oh hell, I screw up many more than I help." I changed my mind about therapy because I did learn of couples who use therapy as a last-ditch effort, and once that fails, they divorce. If they hadn't gone to a therapist at all, sometimes they might stay together knowing that they haven't tried everything yet.

No Therapy at All

In my research on this subject, I've needed to rethink my entire position. I couldn't believe what I learned about cheating men and therapy. You'd think that almost everyone would tap into some form of therapy if they've cheated. Absolutely not. Eighty-three percent of cheating men never went to any form of therapy. What happened? The vast majority never seriously discussed it. With all of the discussion of options that might've ensued, it's perplexing that therapy wasn't one of them. Out of the men who never went to therapy, 70 percent of them never discussed it. Unfortunately, 23 percent of the husbands reported that they had requested it but their wives refused. Only 7 percent of the time did the wives request it and their husbands refused. Is it that therapists have a bad reputation for helping marriages or dealing with infidelity, or that couples are so forlorn and invested in anger that they can't seem to come up for air enough to consider it as a real possibility? From my study, you surely couldn't say it was a result of the therapy failing, because the vast majority didn't even try it.

What about the 17 percent who did go to therapy? Out of that 17 percent, 10 percent went to marital therapy for fewer than three sessions, 6 percent went for three to ten sessions, and sadly only 1 percent went for more than ten sessions. From that 17 percent, 31 percent of the men found the sessions helpful while 69 percent found them generally unproductive. But with only 7 percent out of the entire group going to therapy for more than three sessions, it can't be that therapy is the failure in these cases.

It's possible you could argue that therapy in general doesn't help enough people and therefore people don't consider it. I do know that if you want to protect your marriage and your husband requests marital therapy, you should go with him. Don't be afraid like Maria that somehow you'll be to blame. If that happens, let the therapist know that you feel he or she is making the cheating sound excusable. But get in there and make the effort to create a solid marriage. I'm not necessarily talking about going to therapy only after your husband has cheated. At any point, join your husband in therapy if he makes such a request. To avoid it would be to miss a genuine attempt to make your marriage better, pure and simple, whether or not you believe in therapy.

I've had many people tell me that they don't like or believe in therapy, and I appreciate hearing this feedback because then I can process their concerns. Sometimes they feel therapy is not constructive, because therapists just listen and basically agree with everyone. Sometimes they feel therapists drag things on when there needs to be some deadline for full or partial resolution. By sharing these or any concerns you have with the marriage counselor, you assist the therapist in developing a plan that keeps your needs in mind. I often request that couples give the therapy a three-month intensive trial before making a decision of whether or not they'll stay together. Otherwise, I'm concerned that their lives will be like living in a pressure cooker, reviewing each day's events and wondering whether, they should stay together based on that day. The message is that there is a world of people trained to help marriages who surely can't do so if 93 percent either don't go or bail out in under three sessions.

I found very interesting the statistics gathered from the faithful husbands about the same topic of therapy. More faithful men went to marital therapy than the cheating men. Of the faithful men who said they had marital issues at some point (a large percentage of the whole group reported not going to therapy because their marriage was good enough that therapy was never needed), 25 percent went to therapy compared to 17 percent in the group of cheating men. Most striking is that of this population of faithful men who tapped into therapy, 56 percent found the sessions helpful and only 44 percent found them generally unproductive. That's a 25 percent increase of faithful men finding therapy helpful compared to the cheating men. Forty-four percent of the faithful men never seriously discussed therapy, way down from the 70 percent of cheating men who never seriously discussed it.

We could make a case that because faithful men used therapy more often and when there wasn't any cheating going on, they found it more helpful and it probably contributed to the fact that they indeed remained faithful. Using therapy when you feel things are failing in your marriage seems to be much more of a gain than a potential loss. Don't wait until things are miserable because you believe therapy is for crazy people and peculiar problems. Remember too that therapists are not witch doctors who can see into you or make you reveal what you don't choose to.

Making Marital Counseling Work

People think there are counselors who specialize in marriage counseling or helping couples recover after infidelity. Be aware of what you're asking for. Often, counselors consider themselves specialists in something if they have a lot of experience in it. That's quite a range of definition. There are degrees in some states for a marriage and family counselor, but often this refers to only a minor divergence in their degree where a handful of courses were different from those taken by other therapists. Still, it does say that educationally the therapist has had more coursework than others (although that's not the case for my degree so I'm not tooting my own horn here).

What's with all of the letters after the person's name?

There are psychologists with a doctorate in psychology, who will have the initials PhD or PsyD. Then there are psychiatrists, who are the only ones of the group discussed here who can prescribe medication because they are MDs who have specialized in the human brain. Be aware that many psychiatrists may have had minimal training in marriage counseling; you'll want to ask clearly if they had significant educational training in this area. Then you have each state licensing graduate-level degrees, the most commonly recognized being LCSW (licensed clinical social worker) as well as variations of LMFT (licensed marriage and family therapist) and LMHC (licensed mental health counselor). All of these degrees constitute the proper training to help you and your spouse create a better marriage.

Beware of counseling that doesn't sound right to you or therapists who use New Age techniques that feel uncomfortable, or unethical conduct (I know of one therapist who asked a client to paint his house as a part of therapy). If it doesn't feel right and isn't the norm, then it isn't right for you.

Get a Referral

The best referrals probably come from those who know you. Another couple you're close to whom you know has also had issues and were helped through therapy is a great referral. Your physician would be another. Your mother-in-law? Only if you're really close.

Ask the Right Questions

When you have a phone or in-person conversation with the therapist, do yourself a favor and ask any questions that might help you feel more comfortable. But in the interest of finding the therapist that best suits you from the start, don't give away the answer you want in the question that you ask. Too many people tell the therapist how they want the question answered without realizing it. The therapist, being a trained listener, will then make you feel right at home, giving you the answers and support you need. But in the beginning you need to find out how this therapist works and whether you'll be most comfortable. So when you say, "How do you deal with infidelity? I mean, I don't want somebody who'll excuse it by saying our marriage was bad and that's why it happened," or "Don't you think that if he cheated he should have to lose some of his freedom? How else can I ever trust him again?" the therapist is being told how to answer you. The therapist will respond with something that reassures you that infidelity is wrong and needs to be addressed. You might be surprised that if your husband were to call and say something like, "Do you focus on just the cheating, because I need someone to help us get to the root of our marital problems and my cheating isn't it?" the same therapist might well play down the cheating part for him because that is what he wants to hear. You don't want to find out on session three or four when you've already shared heavily that your therapist is really not in the same ballpark as you and not nearly as sensitive to your issues as you expected. The examples I gave here were about infidelity, but when you're entering counseling with no infidelity in your marriage it can be even more confusing to know how the therapist works. I'm not suggesting that you are supposed to control the therapy, but you just have to find the right chemistry for the therapeutic relationship to work. You'd be better off just asking the questions simply and listening carefully to the answers without letting the therapist know how you feel about the topic. This method can save you a lot of wasted time and your possibly being upset with the therapist because you feel she has changed her tune once therapy is under way.

Create Goals

Most important is that you get clarity from day one. How is this therapist going to help? How long does the therapist think things will take in order to see real growth? The therapist might need a session or two before answering these questions, but you'll feel better knowing the clear direction you're going in. Is this therapist going to give you clear activities and methods to deal with your issues? Is she going to give you enough time to discuss the arguments you have and help both of you to learn to deal with them?

The First Session

Generally, whenever a couple wants to begin marital counseling, I'll request that both come to the first session and I usually require the first session be a double. I want the couple to not only share with me but also have the opportunity to hear what I think I can do in order to help. If one spouse comes alone to the first session, I've found that the spouse who sees me second feels that my objectivity has already been swayed. I'll see that spouse alone if the other spouse refuses to attend at first, but I warn that spouse that I might be compromised as far being able to serve as the marital counselor. I also give each an individual session after the initial session so that each can talk to me very candidly without pulling any punches, and also it gives me an opportunity to explore the deeper voices I've discussed throughout the book. I hope to help the spouses recognize that they are making mistakes they are unaware of because of some of those voices that they've never explored. Also, I create an environment of diplomacy in the first session so that people leave hopeful and not angry because they let loose in the session and made things worse.

Marital counselors have to be in top shape, willing to take control of things and lead your marriage toward positive change. If you leave that first session angry, out of control, and largely directionless, don't waste your time—look for another therapist. Your marriage can't go through a few sessions of bad therapy. Find a better-suited therapist immediately. When you find a great therapist, you should be leaving that first session cautiously hopeful. That's what you're searching for.

APPENDIX B

Healing after an Affair

We've learned what is in your power to best develop a great marriage and prevent an affair. But by the time you read this book you may have already suffered the horrible consequences of cheating. Although there are books dedicated solely to the topic of developing a good marriage after the pain of cheating has occurred, I'll outline the absolutely necessary ingredients for you and your spouse to consider.

Unlike much of this book where I'm speaking to women and explaining what they can do to lead the way to a meaningful marriage, there can't be healing after cheating unless the cheater gets personally involved in the process. The odds of your husband never cheating again go up and down depending upon how involved he is in making the marriage work at this point. If he just wants to apologize, blame it on a midlife crisis, and move on, beware. This is a terrible scenario for you. If he doesn't even think it was such a bad thing and justifies it by proclaiming that all men cheat or he was so displeased with you that what could you expect, it's an even worse scenario. Do I mean it's impossible to make it work and never have your husband cheat again? Nothing's impossible. I just wouldn't want to be the one married to him—and neither would you.

Do I Divorce or Do I Stay?

Be clear on this: only you and your children have to live with the consequences of your decision. Not your parents and not your friends. Only you can decide when to stay and when to leave. And no one needs to judge you. If you want to stay in a marriage where you don't feel you have the security you need after your husband has cheated, you still have the right to stay with him. You can still give it time and see if you can develop something better "for the sake of the kids." But don't tell yourself everything is okay and wonderful when it isn't. Don't put your heart and soul in a vulnerable position unless you are sure things have significantly changed. You can stay as long as you want in your marriage, but if you entrust your husband with your vulnerability and he has not given you reasons to be trusted, then you are making a very unhealthy emotional move. Plug yourself into the Inner Voice Recognition Formula and get some insight immediately. I don't want to be part of any force that tells you to do all the things in my book and commit to change if your husband is either abusive or currently cheating on you. Please do yourself (and your children, if you have them) a favor and go to a therapist. You deserve to take care of yourself.

To any woman who has experienced a husband who's cheated on her, my strongest suggestion is to get professional help. The emotional volatility of an affair makes it very hard for spouses to discuss it properly and move on without the assistance of a trained, objective third person. Please don't use the following guidelines as an alternative to proper psychotherapy but rather as an aid to recreating your relationship.

There are two key ingredients that must be present to properly heal a marriage after an affair:

1. *A remorseful spouse.*   When the spouse who has had an affair doesn't fault himself, there's little point in going further. How can the betrayed partner open up emotionally and become vulnerable to a spouse who doesn't feel he's done anything wrong? Sometimes he might say, "But the marriage was so awful . . ." The answer is that he should have sought help from a therapist or clergyman, or maybe he should have divorced first. Even that would have made this a different scenario. But to blame cheating on anything else other than his own selfish indulgencies will leave you completely distrustful and on such constant alert that you'll never want to sleep with him again.

2. *The certainty that it's over.*   The pain can't begin to heal when your husband is still involved with someone else. Nor can a healthy return to marriage begin. The first issue is helping your straying husband find the motivation and understanding to commit to fully returning to the marriage. This is not always so simple. Many men have fallen in love with a different woman, and even though they say they'd like to make it work with their wives, they feel stuck because they still need the other woman. There is an understandable issue here. If he hasn't already broken it off with the other woman, he might be willing to for the sake of the marriage but he might feel quite sad for some time as he gets "over her." This can be a constant reminder to an already struggling wife. But if it is truly over and he is truly remorseful, it is worth giving it time for him to deal with his sadness and find a renewed, healthier relationship with you.

But if he remains in the least bit involved with the other woman (even just phone calls, still working on projects together at work, "friendly" coffee), then it just ain't over. I never ask any woman in my office to put any effort into connecting with her husband if I know that he is still in some way actively involved with the woman with whom he cheated. How can I ask her to jump hurdles and keep hope and faith without a firm active commitment from her husband? I'm all for one person leading the way but this is not possible under those circumstances. The extramarital relationship must end—physically, emotionally, and sexually.

To the Husband

1. *Apologize.*   When we hurt someone, healing that relationship begins with sincere apologies to the person we hurt. Your ego has no place here. Do not minimize *your* error. Stay away from comments like, "If *you* were more loving, caring, or attentive this never would have happened." I am not saying your point has no validity, but you had an affair and there is no excuse for the betrayal and pain you caused your wife. If your spouse was in fact doing something incorrect or unhealthy, it was part of your marital commitment to do something about it, whether through private discussion or counseling. The moment you decided to add another sexual partner into your marital mix, you were wrong no matter what was going on in your marriage. If there were huge problems in your marriage, you were responsible for creating the opportunity to deal with them. If you chose not to or felt there was no option other than divorce, then you should have waited until you separated and it was clear to your spouse that the marriage was over before you allowed yourself to become intimately involved with another person. This does not mean that there won't be an opportunity for you to discuss what changes you need for this marriage to rebound. That will have to come later as a separate discussion. It can only occur after you profusely apologize and take full responsibility for your mistakes.

2. *Be willing to listen.*   Your wife deserves and needs the opportunity to share her pain. Even if you are extremely remorseful,

your spouse still deserves the opportunity to share with you how horrible the situation was and still is for her even though it may be hard for you to listen to because of how sad it will and should make you feel. Listen intently and empathize with what your spouse is feeling. Set your own hurt feelings aside. Let your spouse know that you understand her feelings and that you would feel the same if she chose to have an affair.

3. *Discuss the affair.*   Your spouse will likely ask a variety of questions about the affair. You may need to share some of the details, but only those that refer to the issue of how the affair came about, and only so you and your spouse can develop a proper precautionary plan for the future. As discussed on page 205, sharing too much can be harmful to the process of going forward. Your wife deserves answers that can be used to develop a plan that will protect her from such behavior in the future.

4. *Change your lifestyle.*   It isn't enough to say, "I'll never do it again." Your wife needs a lot more to go on than a verbal promise. You both need to put thought and energy into understanding how the affair happened and how you will avoid it happening again. Serious limits should be made. You may not like having limits placed on you as if you were a teenager under parental scrutiny, but they are needed to rebuild your wife's trust. What would you do in this area if your wife cheated on you? Most men tell me they'd demand severe scrutiny. Your wife needs no less.

You should be completely transparent in letting your spouse know where you are and what you are doing, and when and why you'll be late returning home. For your wife to be open to you again, she'll need realistic assurances and checks and balances to make sure she is never hurt like this again. Remember the adage "Cheat on me once, shame on you; cheat on me twice, shame on me." It is unreasonable to expect your wife to return to her former trust in you anytime soon after an affair.

5. *Discuss the changes you feel are required from your wife.*   You may have many issues with your wife and feel that they contributed to your having an affair. Never use these need for changes as justification for your affair. But you will need to have the opportunity to discuss these changes with your wife. Again, you should deal with this subject only *after* you've apologized profusely and sincerely heard your partner's pain.

6. *Be prepared to make changes to your life, even if you believe they were not contributors to your cheating.*   When your wife demands that you drop your best friend who has cheated on his wife and kept your cheating a secret, you may feel that your friend had nothing to do with it. The statistics of my study show that cheating men were much more likely to have close friends who cheated than faithful men. Whether or not you agree with your wife's demand, you'll need to listen carefully and make the changes so that she can begin to regain trust. If you're unwilling to make the changes, you're sending a message that the desire not to change that behavior is more important to you than your wife's healing. If you feel her demand is inappropriate (if she asks you never speak to any of your family again, for example), you should bring it up with a counselor.

7. *Commit to a long period of healing.*   Too many offenders think that after a few weeks their spouse should ease up already and stop worrying. You may know in your heart you'd never stray again, but there is no way for your wife to know that other than seeing how you act over time. She has the right to keep a watchful eye out for a long time, commonly a year. It takes many months for a spouse to relax and trust a partner who has had an affair. For some, it takes years before they can await the arrival of a late spouse without first thinking that he is straying again. Respect your spouse's need for reassurance.

8. *Remember that the ultimate trust will be regained through your loving focus.*   When your wife feels you are connected to her and desiring to be her friend and love, that is what will heal and let her offer her trust in you in the future. Read this book and discuss it with her along with other marriage books. Become an expert in marriage in order to show your wife you desire a close, connected relationship. Nothing can ever replace this attitude.

Does One Lie Lead to Another?

When it becomes acceptable to lie about anything it sets a precedent and surely makes it easier to lie and easier to cheat. You may be thinking, "Come on, if he's going to cheat, he's going to cheat, and being honest about whether he was with that friend I can't stand last night at the game won't make any difference." Wrong. Remember, the men in my research were sorry that they had cheated. They weren't "bad" men who were going to cheat no matter what. Eighty-eight percent claimed that had the marriage been different (again, the men would have had to have been part of that difference), they likely would not have cheated.

Lying, deceitfulness, and not correcting misinformation prepare fertile soil for gross lies and deceit.

To avoid making your marriage a hotbed of deception, institute a no-lie policy. This is a struggle for all of us because we all lie. When you ask your husband how your butt looks in that outfit, he better say "fantastic" or else the night is over. Where do we draw the line? Think about it for yourself. Make two lists with the following headings:

Lies I can live with:

Lies I cannot live with:

I help couples use a policy I refer to as Action/Inaction honesty. It means that at the very least there will be complete honesty regarding any action or inaction. If you ask your husband whether he made the deposit and he didn't, that's an inaction, and he's got to be up front with you. If you ask him if he went out with Jerry, his friend whom you hate and have asked him to not go drinking with, he's got to be honest and tell you he did as that is an action taken.

This also means that actions and inactions must be offered up even if not asked if either of you knows the other might be concerned. So although you may have no clue that he spent time with Jerry, he must tell you. This concept of sharing and confronting the issue instead of sweeping it under the rug will force your marriage to deal with the truth. If your husband went to a strip bar, attended a bachelor party that included naked women, got a massage in a parlor that offers "happy endings," it cannot be hidden at any point. As difficult as the truth is, it beats reality distortion hands down and gives you the opportunity to deal with the underlying issue. If you really feel Jerry is the devil incarnate and is dangerous to your husband or marriage, deal with it as a marital issue. You may have to accept that things aren't always as you want them to be, but at least you'll know the truth and be able to handle it as you wish. Obviously, the policy would apply to you in the same way.

What this policy is willing to allow is lies based on opinions—"How do I look? Was sex great for you? What do you think of my mother?"— all questions that we hope we can be honest about but in the reality of life it might be more sensible to fudge the truth (a nicer term for lying). This kind of lying is distinctly different from lying about something you did or did not concretely do. When you lie about an opinion, you don't distort reality nearly the same way as you do when lying about an action or inaction. Also, an important amendment to this rule is that either of you is allowed not to answer when it comes only to an opinion. "I don't want to talk about my opinion of your mother. I'll be nice to her and it'll help if we do this . . ." And perhaps you should stop asking whether you look good in an outfit unless you really want to hear his opinion. Better to ask which outfit he likes better. Or if you're fishing for a compliment, tell him outright, "I love it when you compliment how I look when I get dressed up to go out for the evening."

My research has shown that it is highly unlikely for husbands to admit to cheating unless they are at least faced with evidence. It's worth every effort to develop a marriage that is surrounded by honesty in all parts of your life. This will likely diminish the odds of cheating and surely will allow you to take notice more quickly and easily if your husband if pulling away emotionally or physically. It will help you discover the truth about your husband's marital dissatisfaction or deceitful actions earlier on, possibly avoiding irreparable damage. You'll be able to see if he's telling the truth because he's not used to lying to you previously about real matters and therefore he'll find it harder to lie here as well. He'll know and be used to a marriage in which he can be honest even if he knows it'll upset you. He will be able to come to you earlier on to discuss anything he's doing or not doing that might be the precursor to cheating. This will let you know what's really going on in his life and allow both of you to deal with your issues together instead of waiting until they get out of hand.

Patricia's Story: She Refused the No-Lie Policy

Patricia wasn't keen on the "no-lie" concept. She felt it was childish and unrealistic. She believed her husband's extreme honesty was kind of nerdy. I asked her to try on the Inner Voice Recognition Formula for size.

> *Child voice.*   Patricia felt her parents were honest people. At the same time, there were countless occasions when her mother told her not to tell Dad about the true cost of an item, as her parents fought about money every Sunday when her dad balanced

the checkbook. Patricia told "white lies" on the phone for her mom all the time (especially to Grandma): "She's not home right now," "she's in the shower," "She has a headache." She laughed about an incident when her mom was rushing her out of a grocery store. Patricia, who was about seven, started crying in the car because she thought her mother had stolen some goods. Her mother explained to her what really happened: her mom didn't want to be seen by a friend who was in the store. She had told the friend that morning that she wasn't feeling well and couldn't go out to lunch.

Society voice.   Patricia felt her friends were fairly honest. She didn't think they meant any harm but didn't like the way they'd secretly talk about one another and pretend to be just fine in front of the same person they'd whispered about. Her sister was the queen of that. She'd complain to Patricia about how awful a person was and then invite that same woman out to lunch and include Patricia as well. Patricia couldn't get over how genuinely warm her sister seemed with the same person she was tearing apart on the phone just the day before.

Home voice.   Patricia found her husband to be a straight shooter. He didn't like lying or cheating on taxes. He prided himself on telling it like it is even if it would be easier to lie. Her kids were just in elementary school and were often learning about how important it was to tell the truth.

Insight change.   The end result of her Inner Voice Recognition Formula discovery was that her home was the voice she really had to tap into. Her husband and children supported the no-lie policy, while her first two voices really made her uneasy with it. She recognized that it wasn't worth the risk that came along with lying comfortably in your marriage merely because she had a past that taught her lying was kind of okay.

Inner Voice Recognition Formula: Patricia

Patricia wasn't ready to institute a no-lie policy.

Child voice:
> Her parents were generally honest but told lots of white lies.

> Result: It is ok to lie about "little stuff."

Society voice:
> Her friends gossiped about one another behind one another's backs but pretended everything was wonderful to one another's faces.

> Result: It is normal to be false, even in the company of your friends.

Home voice:
> Her husband was very honest and straitlaced. Her kids learned about honesty in school.

> Result: Her husband set a positive example of honesty although she felt he often went overboard.

Insight change: Patricia's Inner Voice Recognition Formula helped her accept that her husband's being so honest wasn't nerdy. She realized she had been unconsciously following the example of her parents and friends, which she now consciously steered away from. She allowed herself to join her husband's belief system, diminishing her chances of being lied to by him the future and avoiding possible heartbreak.

Find your comfort zone with the white lies but be clear that the action lies are out of bounds. This goes a long way toward securing your marriage.

Your Role as the Wife Who Was Cheated On

The hardest part of this will be for you to identify anything you need to change. When we've been stabbed in the back, we don't often pull the dagger out and wonder what were we doing that allowed it to happen. Self-defense experts, although unwilling to ever blame the victim, will teach you to learn to approach life in such a way that your chances of being attacked are diminished. Once again, even though you are the victim, you need to have a proper understanding of what was going wrong in the marriage before this all happened that possibly made the marriage ripe for some form of failure. Remember that there are those men (12 percent) who cheat for reasons that have nothing to do with what is going on in the marriage. They are just serial cheaters and your odds of healing the marriage are abysmal. But if your husband is remorseful and committed to a marriage of meaningful, consistent connection and you've decided to try to make this work, you will need to confront yourself and see what you've done and what you can do to make your marriage better.

1. *Understand that it was likely that your marriage was suffering.* There were things you weren't doing (perhaps not working hard enough on making the marriage better or not pushing to see a marital counselor), and this may well have contributed to the strain on your marriage. Forget for a moment the fact that your husband cheated. The best way to look at this is to imagine that he came to you and said, "I need a separation." Then it would become your collective charge to seek help and figure out a way to repair this. But the key to healing and creating a renewed protected marriage is consistent focus and effort on your marital relationship—and that includes both of you. At this point, it's the only way. You can protect yourself by telling him he has to be the one to lead the way and you'll respond to his gestures. But he will need to see that his gestures are receiving some response or else he will become hopeless. This is a hard one because many women quite understandably don't want to have to respond. If you just don't have it in you, let him know he shouldn't be trying right now because you're just not ready to receive any loving gesture from him yet. But make it your priority to get to the place

internally where you can receive them as soon as possible. The likelihood is that time is running out.

2. *Be ready to change.*   Be brutally honest with yourself about your own flaws. Be willing and ready to hear your husband's feelings and needs. This should only come after much apologizing and commitment to change from him. Do not allow him to use your flaws or the problems in the marriage as justification for his cheating. If you do, your odds for being cheated on again go up. As much as your spouse must be willing to make lifestyle changes to reassure you he won't ever stray again, you'll need to make changes as well. Once he shows he's changing, it'll be easier for you to do the same. After all, what use is it to return to the way it was, which obviously was flawed for your husband, and most likely for you as well? Create some new clear-cut ideas on paper as I've done in my Quick Action Program throughout this book.

3. *Limit your questions.*   You're going to want to know details, and it wouldn't be uncommon for you to be agitated until you receive every answer. Some wives claim it helps them move through the pain. For the most part, I feel it prolongs the pain and creates deep scars. It's the difference between reading about something horrific and seeing it. The more details you know, the more graphic imagery you will have, and those images will seriously decrease your ability to forget the past and focus on the future.

On the other hand, there are some questions you are entitled to know the answers to, as a means of developing a marital plan for the future and learning to trust your spouse again. The answers to these questions will help you determine how to move forward with a plan to help you trust your husband:

- Who is the other woman?
- How/where did you meet?

- How long has this relationship been going on?
- Do you have any relationship with her now or do you foresee having one in the future?
- Did anyone else know about your affair? Who?
- What was happening in your head that would allow you to do this?

   This last one is important to ask, but be clear that you're going to get a justification. He's going to say the wrong thing like, "My buddies do it," "You were so angry at me," or "You were driving me crazy." But you asked him what was going on in his head at the time, not how he now understands it. However, you do want to know what was in his mind because it'll lead you to better understand your husband. The first answer tells you he better stay away from his so-called buddies. The second answer tells you he had difficulty dealing with your anger. Remember, your anger might have been justified at the time and perhaps it wasn't as bad as you thought. But the fact that he had it in his mind as a rationalization tells you that's an area the marriage has to focus on repairing. The same goes for answer number three. Perhaps you had a right to annoy him or you don't think you were annoying him. The issue is that your new relationship will have to take this area into serious account and work on it at length to find the proper solution.

   Ask any question that will help you form a plan for security and trust for the future. However, there are many unproductive questions that you may also want the answers to. They tend to revolve around the details of activities and personal information of the other person:

- How often did you have sex?
- What was the sex like?
- Was it better with her than when we have sex?

- Do you think she's more beautiful/smart/sexy than me?
- What does she have that I don't?

I'm not suggesting that you're not entitled to any answer you want. But keep this in mind: the answers to these questions will likely torment you, and none of them will make you feel any better. If he's truly being honest what do expect him to say? The sex was horrible, he couldn't get you out of his mind the whole time. The other woman was a cross between a mutt and a bus. The answers will be based on your husband's wrongdoing and unhealthy behavior. If he has already admitted it was wrong and decided to return to a life with you, then get to the two of you as soon as possible. Make new memories and don't work to visualize the details of the ugly parts of the past. No matter how great the affair may have been, your spouse has chosen to be with you. The reason behind that decision may not be the one you'd ideally like— for the kids, for example—but it's strong enough to pull your spouse away from whatever he saw in this other person. Some piece of that has to be his desire to make it work with you. The more details you know, the more difficult it will be for you to love your spouse. You don't want to have an image of him having sex with another woman every time the two of make love. Be kind to yourself and deal with the realistic issues at hand.

4. *Don't bring up the affair again and again.*   Your spouse can only apologize so many times without becoming frustrated. You want a genuine apology and the reassurances that it will never recur. It is difficult enough for anyone to admit to his error, apologize, and be sensitive to how his behavior hurt another. You will need to hear him apologize repeatedly. But if you constantly bring up the affair, it's simply unfair. It sucks energy out of the new commitment, and unless you have a good reason—something he's done today that reminds you of his behavior during the affair, for example—stop

yourself from going back to it again and again. No jabs, digs, eye movements when out with friends discussing fidelity. If you feel a need to remind your husband of the affair because you feel he's behaving in a way that could lead to another affair, get immediate counseling. But to remind your spouse of the affair in the midst of an argument as a punitive tool will damage your ability to communicate honestly as a couple. You could say you can't control it because you're so angry. Deal with your anger in a healthy way; otherwise this marriage is spinning its wheels.

5. *Resolve to move on.*   There is no magic to forgiveness. It is the strength of the human mind and heart to forgive and create a new life together with your spouse. If you are satisfied with the new plan to prevent future cheating and create a better marriage, your job is to let go of the past. Look into the future and see you and your spouse happily married years from now.

Finally, sometimes separation is indicated after cheating. Just because you're choosing to get through this and your husband is apologetic does not mean you have to immediately return to being husband and wife. You may need time to see him make some genuine changes before you move forward with him. You may not want to live together, have sex (be sure to have him tested for sexually transmitted diseases before you have any form of unprotected sex regardless of how "protected" he claims his cheating sex was), or even make physical contact for some time.

Remember, though, that it becomes counterproductive to put the marriage on ice for too long without expecting it to result in two people who are cold to each other. Get help to make a plan, and as you see your spouse proving his renewed commitment to the marriage and fidelity, get back in the game and get to winning for him and for you.

RECOMMENDED READING

Brizendine, Louann. *The Female Brain*. New York: Broadway Books, 2006.

Druckerman, Pamela. *Lust in Translation: The Rules of Infidelity from Tokyo to Tennessee*. New York: Penguin Press, 2007.

Glass, Shirley, and Jean Coppock Staeheli. *Not "Just Friends": Rebuilding Trust and Recovering Your Sanity after Infidelity*. New York: Free Press, 2004.

Gottman, John M., and Nan Silver. *The Seven Principles for Making a Marriage Work: A Practical Guide from the Country's Foremost Relationship Expert*. New York: Crown Publishers, 1999.

Hillman, Carolynn. *Recovery of Your Self-Esteem: A Guide for Women*. New York: Fireside, 1992.

Juan, Stephen. *The Odd Brain: Mysteries of Our Weird and Wonderful Brains Explained*. Sydney: HarperCollins Australia, 1999.

Lieberman, David J. *Never Be Lied to Again: How to Get the Truth in 5 Minutes or Less in Any Conversation or Situation*. New York: St. Martin's Press, 1999.

Lusterman, Don-David. *Infidelity: A Survival Guide*. New York: MJF Books, 1999.

Miller, Alice. *The Drama of the Gifted Child: The Search for the True Self*. New York: Basic Books, 1997.

Pittmann, Frank. *Private Lies: Infidelity and the Betrayal of Intimacy*. New York: W.W. Norton & Company, 1990.

Webb, Michael. *The RoMANtics Guide: Hundreds of Creative Tips for a Lifetime of Love*. New York: Hyperion, 2000.

INDEX

acquaintances, influence of, 34.
See also friends
Action/Inaction honesty,
199–203
ADD, 164
affairs. *See* healing of marriage;
men; mistresses; research
Andrews, Cecile, 83
antidepressants, 163
anxiety, 164
apologizing, 152–153, 196,
207–208
appreciation, 25
apologizing by husband and,
152–153
criticism by husband and,
46–47
criticism of husband and, 125
emotional dissatisfaction of
husband and, 20–24
exercise for, 22–23
expressing, as problematic,
120–123

husband's response to,
66–70
Inner Voice Recognition
Formula example,
120–123
See also gestures; Quick
Action Program
avoidant behavior, 43–47

bathroom behavior, 109–110
beds/bedding, 168
Berk, Lee, 167
birth control, 111
body image, 36, 93–94
brain
memory exercises for, 169
perception of personal
history, 117–118 (*See also*
Inner Voice Recognition
Formula)
breadwinner role, 24–25
Brizendine, Louann, 16
Byrne, Rhonda, 181

"society voice," 119, 120
    appreciation and, 122
    compassion and, 128
    healing and, 202
    resentment and, 131
    sex life and, 137–138, 142, 146
    successful marriages and, 158
    See also Inner Voice
        Recognition Formula
stimulants, 164
stress, 164
sunlight, 167

Tallmadge, Katherine, 168
therapists
    credentials of, 189–190
    interviewing, 190–191
    referrals for, 190
    See also marriage counseling
Thoreau, Henry David, 167
thoughtfulness. *See* gestures
touch
    communicating and, 80
    importance of, 179
trust
    importance of, 6, 9
    regaining, 199

See also healing of marriage;
    lying

vacation, importance of, 169
vibrators, 101–102

warm and thoughtful gestures.
    See gestures
warning signs. *See* signals of
    infidelity
water, relaxation benefits from,
    167
WebMD.com (Web site), 100
"white lies," 199–203
Why Do Men Cheat?
    (questionnaire), 11–14
womansavers.com
    (Web site), 19
work/life balance, 82–85
    compartmentalization and,
        74–76
    men in breadwinner role and,
        24–25
    men's changing roles and,
        22–24
workplace, initiation of affairs
    in, 55–56

ABOUT THE AUTHOR

M. Gary Neuman is a Florida state-licensed mental health counselor, a rabbi, and the creator of the internationally recognized Sandcastles program for children of divorce. He and his work have been featured multiple times on *Oprah, The View, Today*, and National Public Radio's *Talk of the Nation*, as well as on *Good Morning America, NBC Nightly News, CBS Weekend News*, and *Dateline NBC*. Neuman's work has been featured in *People, Time, Cosmopolitan*, the *Washington Post*, the *Chicago Tribune*, the *Miami Herald*, and the *Los Angeles Times*. He is a member of the Advisory Board for *Parents* magazine, and his international column "Changing Families" has won numerous awards, including the Parenting Publications of America Award of Excellence.

Neuman tours the country speaking about marital and family issues. He maintains a private practice in Miami where he also offers his 2 × 2 Relationship Seminars, a unique, intensive all-day counseling program for couples. He lives with his wife and five children in Miami Beach.

If you would like to find more information or contact Gary Neuman, please write to:

M. Gary Neuman, LMHC
P.O. Box 402691
Miami Beach, FL 33140-0691
You can also visit his Web site at www.mgaryneuman.com.